T0329526

AGGREGATION IN ECONOMIC ANALYSIS
An Introductory Survey

AGGREGATION
IN ECONOMIC ANALYSIS
An Introductory Survey

BY

H. A. JOHN GREEN

PRINCETON UNIVERSITY PRESS
PRINCETON, NEW JERSEY
1964

❖

Publication of this book
has been aided by the Ford Foundation program
to support publication,
through university presses, of work in the
humanities and social sciences.

❖

Printed in the United States of America
by
The William Byrd Press, Inc.
Richmond, Virginia

TO B, C AND D

Preface

My interest in the problem of aggregation began when, in the course of a study of growth models, I became disturbed by Mrs. Robinson's criticisms of her professional colleagues for their failure to state how they were assuming capital to be measured. These criticisms led me to try to find out what economists had said about the measurement of economic quantities in general, and particularly of those quantities which represented by a single number a collection of heterogeneous objects.

I found that the attitude of many economists to this problem seemed to resemble that of the Scottish preacher whom Sir Dennis Robertson quotes as saying to his flock, "Brethren, here is a gr-reat difficulty; let us look it firmly in the face and pass on." Of those who had stayed to wrestle with the difficulty, on the other hand, many appeared to be unaware of the results of contests which seemed to me to be of a nature similar to their own.

These findings induced me to attempt to uncover some of the basic propositions underlying the theory of aggregation in general, and to show the relationships existing among a variety of contributions to the field. Two aspects of the subject have perhaps received insufficient emphasis in the following pages. In the first place, differentiable functions have been assumed nearly everywhere; this gives the work an almost old-fashioned flavour, though one in keeping with the bulk of the literature. The aggregation problems of activity analysis (a taste is to be found at the very end of Chapter 9) might make an interesting field of study. In the second place, I have ventured only a little way into the somewhat unfamiliar region of statistical theory, though I have tried to emphasize in the later parts of the volume the great importance of the statistical aspects of the aggregation problem.

Work was begun in the summer of 1959 at the Ford Foundation Regional Faculty Research Seminar in Economics in Berkeley, California, and continued during the summer of 1960 with the help of a grant from the Social Science Research Council, and during the summers of 1961 and 1962 with the help of grants from the Canada Council. The assistance given by these institutions is greatly appreciated. I owe a special debt to Professor A. G. Papandreou, who was the director of the seminar in Berkeley in 1959, for the advice and instruction I received from him then, and for the encouragement he has given me since that time.

I am of course greatly indebted to the many authors in the field from whose works I have borrowed. To the acknowledgements in the text

I must add two more. One is to Professor William C. Hood, whom I am fortunate to have as a colleague, and from whom I have learnt a great deal in our discussions. The other is to Professor Paul A. Samuelson; my debt to him can be fully appreciated only by those who have shared the privilege of being taught by him.

To my wife, for her constant encouragement and great forbearance through the four long summers during which this book was written, I can find no adequate words to say.

Toronto   H.A.J.G.
November, 1962

Contents

Part I
INTRODUCTION

CHAPTER 1

The Problem of Aggregation

In the broadest sense, aggregation is a process whereby a part of the information available for the solution of a problem is sacrificed for the purpose of making the problem more easily manageable. We shall be concerned in this volume with the cases in which aggregation takes the form of replacing a set of numbers (for instance, quantities or prices of commodities) by a single number or a smaller set of numbers or "aggregates" (for instance, quantity or price indices). Aggregation will be judged satisfactory by the economist to the extent that he believes that the cost of handling information in greater detail outweighs the greater reliability of the results he might obtain by using more detailed information; the judgment must depend, of course, on the purpose of the investigator.

It must be admitted that the bulk of the literature on aggregation has not been concerned with the comparison of these two kinds of cost—the cost of handling and the cost of sacrificing detailed information. Most writers appear to have been mainly interested in discovering the conditions in which "consistent" aggregation (to use McManus' term) is possible. Aggregation will be said to be consistent when the use of information more detailed than that contained in the aggregates would make no difference to the results of the analysis of the problem at hand.

To illustrate the concept of consistent aggregation, let us assume that each household's consumption is a function of its income alone. Let us define aggregate income as the sum of household incomes and aggregate consumption as the sum of household consumptions. In what conditions is aggregate consumption as defined a function of (that is, uniquely determined by) aggregate income? If there are no restrictions on the distribution of income, the necessary and sufficient condition is that all marginal propensities to consume are constant and equal (see Chap. 5 below). If the only concern of the investigator is to predict aggregate consumption, this property of the marginal propensities ensures that the aggregation procedure described is consistent; knowledge of the distribution of income, for example, would not affect the result of his analysis.

Now it is in fact always possible to define aggregates of such a kind that aggregation is consistent. In the consumption example, if there are only two households with incomes $4683 and $6125 and consumptions $3871 and $5019 respectively, we can define aggregate income as 46836125 and aggregate consumption as 38715019! "Aggregation" will then be consistent, but in fact no aggregation has been performed

3

because none of the information available has been sacrificed. (Cf. the discussion of Theil's "perfect" aggregation in Chap. 5 below, p. 41).

The view has recently been expressed that the problem of aggregation as defined above is of no great importance; see Peston (1959).[1] Peston argues (p. 61): "If the macro-theory were valid, any micro-theory invented to explain the same universe would be either otiose or wrong." Now it must be admitted that the micro-theory may be wrong in a way which has an important bearing on the problem of aggregation. In the consumption problem discussed earlier, suppose that each household's consumption depends not only on its own income but also on the total income. Then a "micro-theory" which neglects this latter dependence contains a specification error; it may even be that predictions based on the aggregate equation are more accurate than those based on the individual household equations (cf. the paper by Grunfeld and Griliches (1960) discussed in Chap. 12 below).

But if no specification error exists, or if it is corrected, in the individual equations, are aggregate theories usually so satisfactory as to leave no room for significant improvement? Might not indications gleaned from micro-theory concerning aggregation bias (Chap. 12 below), or concerning the desirability of including additional variables (Chap. 8 below), in the aggregate equation, be of assistance to the investigator?

We proceed on the assumption that the problem of aggregation is important, and that a survey of the contributions of those who share this view is useful. The greater part of this survey is concerned with the following type of problem. Given (1) an economic relationship or set of relationships expressing one variable as a function of a set of independent variables, (2) an aggregation procedure, more or less well-defined, (3) a relationship, more or less well-defined, among the aggregates: what are the necessary and sufficient conditions for consistent aggregation as defined above? Part II of this work analyzes the problem of grouping variables in a single equation, and relies heavily on the Sono-Leontief concept of "functional separability." Part III is concerned with the aggregation of equations, a problem which arises in connection with market demand functions, aggregate production functions, community preference fields, and the consolidation of sectors in input-output analysis. Part IV is devoted to the particular problems involved in aggregative models of economic growth, with special reference to the measurement of capital, and draws heavily on earlier parts of the work.

In all these cases, if nothing is known about the behaviour of the independent variables, the assumption of consistent aggregation imposes severe restrictions on the individual functions. These restrictions become

[1] When the name of an author is followed by a date in parentheses, details of the work referred to will be found in the list of references, pp. 121–26 below.

4

less severe if the behaviour of the "independent" variables is itself restricted (e.g. if the distribution of incomes is fixed, or changes systematically). The nature of the individual functions, or the behaviour of the independent variables, may permit consistent aggregation to be achieved by the introduction of additional variables into the aggregate equation (Chaps. 5 and 8 below), although the improvement in results must be weighted against the cost of handling a larger number of variables.

In Part V, the errors resulting from aggregation are discussed. No account of aggregation which confines itself to the derivation of the precise conditions for consistent aggregation can be regarded as complete. Indications as to the sources of error and their probable magnitude are essential if alternative aggregation procedures are to be evaluated. In Chapter 12 some of the statistical aspects of the aggregation problem are discussed, and Chapter 13 is an account of some of the special difficulties involved in the concept of an aggregate production function. Part VI summarizes, with references to the text, the considerations involved in the selection of an appropriate form of aggregation.

We conclude this introduction with a brief comment on earlier general treatments of the aggregation problem. A short but penetrating discussion is contained in Chapter VI of Samuelson (1947). Theil's book (1954) is a standard work; it may perhaps be regarded as pioneering in the field rather than surveying it. Allen (1956, Chap. 20) gives a useful summary of the core of Theil's work. Morishima (1961) gives a brief survey of part of the field; Gorman (1959a) shows the connections among a number of contributions, and expresses the view (1959b) that analysis of the underlying mathematical structure of the aggregation problem is desirable. A profound and original paper by Malinvaud (1956a), unfortunately somewhat inaccessible, is strongly recommended.

Part II

GROUPING OF VARIABLES IN A SINGLE UTILITY OR PRODUCTION FUNCTION

CHAPTER 2
The Concept of Functional Separability

1.

In the theory of demand and the theory of production it is commonly assumed that the household or firm purchases that collection of commodities or inputs which maximizes utility or output subject to a budget constraint. The number of different commodities or inputs, distinguishable by their nature, brand or quality, is generally so large that considerable interest attaches to the conditions in which it is possible to reduce the number of variables by grouping together some of the commodities or inputs, representing the quantities and prices of the members of each group by a quantity-index and a price-index.

Now it is possible to argue that no two commodity units or input units can be alike in all respects (for example, they cannot occupy the same space at the same time!). Insistence on this point would, of course, destroy all marginal analysis in economics. We shall assume throughout this volume that, in any applications of the theories discussed, there is a degree of disaggregation at which it is legitimate to assume the perfect substitutability of elements treated as units of a given commodity or input. We shall call those elements units of "elementary" commodities or inputs, and assume that the marginal analysis can be applied to utility or production functions which have elementary commodities or inputs as their arguments.

Elementary commodities or inputs can of course be grouped in a variety of ways. But let us suppose that the following procedure for maximizing utility or output is available. The elementary variables are grouped, and for each group a price-index is defined as a function of the prices of members of the group. First, the optimal distribution of a given total expenditure among the groups is determined by reference to the price-indices alone. The expenditure thus allocated to each group is then distributed among the members of the group on the basis of their individual prices. Moreover, the quantity of each elementary commodity or input determined by this "two-stage" procedure is identical with the amount which would have been purchased if utility or output, regarded as a function of all the elementary variables, had been maximized with reference to all the individual prices, without any grouping. The "aggregation" of the elementary variables into groups is then "consistent," according to the definition of consistency given in Chapter 1. The remainder of Part II is concerned with the conditions for consistent grouping of variables in this sense.

We shall, however, introduce into the analysis a more stringent condition. If the two-stage maximization procedure is possible, group quantity indices can be defined in such a way that utility or output may be written as a function of such indices. But they can not necessarily be defined in such a way that the product of the quantity-index and the price-index for a group equals expenditure on that group. Now applications of the theory of demand and the theory of production admit a small number of variables—fewer than would be necessary if the variables were strictly elementary commodities or inputs. The theory treats these variables as if they were elementary commodities or inputs, whereas they are properly to be regarded as quantity-indices. The product of the quantity and the price of an elementary commodity or input equals the expenditure on it. It follows that strict justification of the grouping of variables requires not only a justification of the two-stage maximization procedure, but also the possibility of defining for each group a quantity-index which, when multiplied by the group price-index, gives the expenditure on members of the group.

The analysis of the two-stage maximization procedure is the work of Strotz (1957, 1959) and Gorman (1959a). It relies heavily on the concept of "functional separability," developed independently by Sono (1961) and Leontief (1947a, 1947b), to which we now turn.

2.

Consider the function:

$$y = f(x_{11}, \cdots, x_{1n_1}, \cdots, x_{r1}, \cdots, x_{rk},$$
$$\cdots, x_{rn_r}, \cdots, x_{m1}, \cdots, x_{mn_m}) \qquad (2.1)$$

whose arguments are all non-negative, in number $N = \sum_{r=1}^{m} n_r$. The function f is assumed to have the following properties:

(a) For all $r, k(r = 1, \cdots, m; k = 1, \cdots, n_r)$:

$$\frac{\partial f}{\partial x_{rk}} > 0 \qquad (2.2)$$

(b) The principal minors of order p $(p \geqq 3)$ of the determinant:

$$D = \begin{bmatrix} 0 & f_{11} & \cdots & f_{rk} & \cdots & f_{mn_m} \\ f_{11} & f_{11 \cdot 11} & \cdots & f_{11 \cdot rk} & \cdots & f_{11 \cdot mn_m} \\ \cdots & \cdots & \cdots & \cdots & \cdots & \cdots \\ f_{rk} & f_{rk \cdot 11} & \cdots & f_{rk \cdot rk} & \cdots & f_{rk \cdot mn_m} \\ \cdots & \cdots & \cdots & \cdots & \cdots & \cdots \\ f_{mn_m} & f_{mn_m \cdot 11} & \cdots & f_{mn_m \cdot rk} & \cdots & f_{mn_m \cdot mn_m} \end{bmatrix} \qquad (2.3)$$

have the sign of $(-1)^{p+1}$, where $f_{rk} = \partial f/\partial x_{rk}$ and $f_{rk \cdot qj} = \partial^2 f/\partial x_{rk}\partial x_{qj}$.

The function f may be regarded either as a utility function or as a production function. The variables x_{rk} are "elementary" commodities or inputs as defined above. Property (a) says that the marginal utility of each commodity or the marginal physical product of each input is always positive. Property (b) implies that the satisfaction of the first-order conditions for a maximum of y, subject to the budget constraint $\sum_{r=1}^{m} \sum_{k=1}^{n_r} p_{rk}x_{rk} \leqq E$, will yield a maximum; property (b) embodies what are commonly called the Hicksian stability conditions (see Hicks (1946) pp. 25, 306).

Our first task is to seek the conditions in which (2.1) may be written as

$$y = F(x_1, \cdots, x_r, \cdots, x_m) \tag{2.4}$$

where for each r $(r = 1, \cdots, m)$

$$x_r = f_r(x_{r1}, \cdots, x_{rk}, \cdots, x_{rn_r}) \tag{2.5}$$

Before we state and prove the main theorem of this chapter, we shall present a heuristic argument based on a simple case considered by Solow (1956b). Let output, Q, be a function of labour, L, and two kinds of capital goods, C_1 and C_2. We wish to write output as a function only of labour and "capital," C, where C is a function of C_1 and C_2.

Let us hold the amount of labour constant at 100 units, and agree to represent two combinations of C_1 and C_2 by the same value of C if and only if, when used with 100 units of labour, they yield equal outputs. Thus, if the following figures are consistent with the production function, we shall say that $C(20, 5) = C(18, 6)$.

L	C_1	C_2	Q
100	20	5	1000
100	18	6	1000

If we change the amount of labour to 200 units, we may find the following figures:

L	C_1	C_2	Q
200	20	5	1800
200	18	6	1700

If we adopt the same rule as before for assigning values to the capital index, we must now say that $C(20, 5) \neq C(18, 6)$. From consideration of the production function, there appears to be no basis for the construction of a capital index. Such an index can be constructed only if any two combinations of C_1 and C_2 that yield equal outputs when used with one quantity of labour also yield equal outputs when used with any other quantity of labour. Some such relationship as the following must therefore hold:

L	C_1	C_2	Q
200	20	5	1800
200	18	6	1800

The marginal rate of substitution of $2C_1$ for $1C_2$ must always hold between the points $(20, 5)$ and $(18, 6)$, irrespective of the amount of labour employed.[1]

3.

The following theorem is due to Leontief (1947a, 1947b):

THEOREM 1: *The necessary and sufficient conditions for equation* (2.1) *to be expressible in the form* (2.4), *where each x_r can be written in the form* (2.5) *and the variables x_{rk} may take any non-negative values, are that:*

For all r, j, $k(r = 1, \cdots, m; j, k = 1, \cdots, n_r)$

$$\frac{\partial f}{\partial x_{rj}} \bigg/ \frac{\partial f}{\partial x_{rk}} = f_{r \cdot jk}(x_{r1}, \cdots, x_{rn_r})$$

or equivalently
For all q, r, i, j, $k(q, r = 1, \cdots, m : q \neq r; i = 1, \cdots, n_q; j, k = 1, \cdots, n_r)$

$$\frac{\partial}{\partial x_{qi}} \left(\frac{\partial f}{\partial x_{rj}} \bigg/ \frac{\partial f}{\partial x_{rk}} \right) = 0.$$

The theorem says that it is a necessary and sufficient condition for the grouping of variables (or their "functional separability," to use Leontief's term[2]), that the marginal rate of substitution between any two variables in a group shall be a function only of the variables in that group, and therefore independent of the value of any variable in any other group.

We pause to point out that when we say that y is a *function* of the elementary variables $x_{11}, \cdots, x_{rk}, \cdots, x_{mn_m}$, we mean that the function f assigns a *unique* value of y to each combination of values of the elementary variables. We seek the conditions in which there exist functions $f_r(r = 1, \cdots, m)$ which assign unique values of x_r to given values of $x_{r1}, \cdots, x_{rn_r}$, and a function F which assigns a unique value of y to given values of $x_1, \cdots, x_m$, so that

$$f(x_{11}, \cdots, x_{rk}, \cdots, x_{mn_m}) = F(x_1, \cdots, x_m)$$
$$= F[x_1(x_{11}, \cdots, x_{1n_1}), \cdots, x_r(x_{r1}, \cdots, x_{rn_r}), \cdots, x_m(x_{m1}, \cdots, x_{mn_m})].$$

Now it is plainly a necessary condition for the existence of such functions that all possible *changes* in the variables x_{rk} lead to *equal*

---

[1] The foregoing argument has been based on the assumption that the behaviour of C_1 and C_2 is unrestricted. If their quantities or prices always move proportionally, however, an index can be readily constructed (see Ch. 4 below).

[2] The interpretation of the term here corresponds to what has come to be called "weak separability" (cf. below, p. 22).

changes in the values of the functions f and F; that is, that $dy = df \equiv dF$. If in addition we can show that $f = F$ for *one* set of values of the variables x_{rk}, then $df \equiv dF$ implies that $f = F$ for all such sets of values, and the necessary conditions are also sufficient.

These considerations will be of help in the proofs of many of the theorems to follow. Bearing them in mind, we may proceed to the proof of Theorem 1.

Proof of Theorem 1:

(i) *Necessity*

Theorem 1 implies that, for all values of the variables x_{rk},

$$df = \sum_{r-1}^{m} \sum_{k-1}^{n_r} \frac{\partial f}{\partial x_{rk}} \, dx_{rk} \equiv dF = \sum_{r-1}^{m} \frac{\partial F}{\partial x_r} \, dx_r$$

$$= \sum_{r-1}^{m} \sum_{k-1}^{n_r} \frac{\partial F}{\partial x_r} \frac{\partial x_r}{\partial x_{rk}} \, dx_{rk}.$$

Hence for all $r, j, k (r = 1, \cdots, m; j, k = 1, \cdots, n_r)$

$$\frac{\partial f}{\partial x_{rj}} = \frac{\partial F}{\partial x_r} \frac{\partial x_r}{\partial x_{rj}}; \qquad \frac{\partial f}{\partial x_{rk}} = \frac{\partial F}{\partial x_r} \frac{\partial x_r}{\partial x_{rk}}$$

so that

$$\frac{\partial f}{\partial x_{rj}} \bigg/ \frac{\partial f}{\partial x_{rk}} = \frac{\partial x_r}{\partial x_{rj}} \bigg/ \frac{\partial x_r}{\partial x_{rk}}$$

But since x_r is a function only of the variables $x_{r1}, \cdots, x_{rn_r}$, the same must be true of its partial derivatives, of the ratios of its partial derivatives, and of any expression which is identically equal to such a ratio. It follows, as required, that

$$\frac{\partial f}{\partial x_{rj}} \bigg/ \frac{\partial f}{\partial x_{rk}} = f_{r \cdot jk}(x_{r1}, \cdots, x_{rn_r})$$

(ii) *Sufficiency*

We now show that the necessary conditions are also sufficient.

Consider a particular vector of values of the variables in the 2nd, 3rd, $\cdots$, m^{th} groups; say $(x'_{21}, \cdots, x'_{rk}, \cdots, x'_{mn_m})$. Let us construct a partition[3] of the set of vectors of values of variables in the first group in such a way that two such vectors $(x'_{11}, \cdots, x'_{1n_1})$ and $(x''_{11}, \cdots, x''_{1n_1})$ belong to the same element of the partition if and only if

$$f(x'_{11}, \cdots, x'_{1n_1}, x'_{21}, \cdots, x'_{rk}, \cdots, x'_{mnm})$$

$$= f(x''_{11}, \cdots, x''_{1n_1}, x'_{21}, \cdots, x'_{rk}, \cdots, x'_{mn m}).$$

[3] A *partition* of a set S is a set whose elements are subsets of S, with the property that each element of S belongs to one and only one element of the partition.

Consider now a second vector of values of variables in groups other than the first, $(x''_{21}, \cdots, x''_{rk}, \cdots, x''_{mn_m})$, and a second partition of the vectors of the first group, so constructed that $(x'_{11}, \cdots, x'_{1n_1})$ and $(x''_{11}, \cdots, x''_{1n_1})$ belong to the same element of the second partition if and only if

$$f(x'_{11}, \cdots, x'_{1n_1}, x''_{21}, \cdots, x''_{rk}, \cdots, x''_{mn_m})$$
$$= f(x''_{11}, \cdots, x''_{1n_1}, x''_{21}, \cdots, x''_{rk}, \cdots, x''_{mn_m}).$$

We shall show that, if the necessary conditions derived above are satisfied, the two partitions must be identical. For if this were not so, there would be a pair of vectors of values of the first group of variables which belonged to the same element of one partition but to different elements of the other. This would imply that

$$f(x'_{11}, \cdots, x'_{1n_1}, x'_{21}, \cdots, x'_{rk}, \cdots, x'_{mn_m})$$
$$= f(x''_{11}, \cdots, x''_{1n_1}, x'_{21}, \cdots, x'_{rk}, \cdots, x'_{mn_m}) \tag{2.6}$$

$$f(x'_{11}, \cdots, x'_{1n_1}, x''_{21}, \cdots, x''_{rk}, \cdots, x''_{mn_m})$$
$$\neq f(x''_{11}, \cdots, x''_{1n_1}, x''_{21}, \cdots, x''_{rk}, \cdots, x''_{mn_m}). \tag{2.7}$$

Since the function f has been implicitly assumed to be continuous, it follows from (2.6) that it is possible, holding the values of variables in groups other than the first constant at $(x'_{21}, \cdots, x'_{rk}, \cdots, x'_{mn_m})$, to move along a continuous path (in an indifference surface or an iso-product surface) from the point $(x'_{11}, \cdots, x'_{1n_1})$ to the point $(x''_{11}, \cdots, x''_{1n_1})$, maintaining a constant value of y throughout. But (2.7) implies that a movement along the same path, but with other variables held constant at $(x''_{21}, \cdots, x''_{rk}, \cdots, x''_{mn_m})$ would not leave the value of y unchanged. There must be a stage on the path, say at the point $(\overline{x}_{11}, \cdots, \overline{x}_{1n_1})$, where

$$f(\overline{x}_{11} + dx_{11}, \cdots, \overline{x}_{1n_1} + dx_{1n_1}, x'_{21}, \cdots, x'_{mn_m})$$
$$- f(\overline{x}_{11}, \cdots, \overline{x}_{1n_1}, x'_{21}, \cdots, x'_{mn_m}) = 0; \tag{2.8}$$

$$f(\overline{x}_{11} + dx_{11}, \cdots, \overline{x}_{1n_1} + dx_{1n_1}, x''_{21}, \cdots, x''_{mn_m})$$
$$- f(\overline{x}_{11}, \cdots, \overline{x}_{1n_1}, x''_{21}, \cdots, x''_{mn_m}) \neq 0. \tag{2.9}$$

In the first case (2.8)

$$dy = \sum_{k=1}^{n_1} \frac{\partial f}{\partial x_{1k}} dx_{1k} = 0$$

so that, since $\partial f / \partial x_{1k} > 0$ for all k (by (2.2) above)

$$dx_{11} + \sum_{k=2}^{n_1} \frac{\partial f}{\partial x_{1k}} \Big/ \frac{\partial f}{\partial x_{11}} dx_{1k} = 0.$$

In the second case (2.9), $dy \neq 0$, so that

$$dx_{11} + \sum_{k=2}^{n_1} \frac{\partial f}{\partial x_{1k}} \Big/ \frac{\partial f}{\partial x_{11}} dx_{1k} \neq 0.$$

The values of $x_{11}, dx_{11}, \cdots, x_{1n_1}, dx_{1n_1}$ are the same in each case. The ratios $(\partial f / \partial x_{1k})/(\partial f / \partial x_{11})$ depend, by the necessary conditions, only on the values of $x_{11}, \cdots, x_{1n_1}$. Hence dy must be the same in each case. Since it is not, the hypothesis that the two partitions are different must be rejected.

Similar arguments would show that a unique partition can be constructed for each group of variables. We now assign to each element of each partition a unique real number x_r, in such a way that no two distinct elements of a partition have the same real number, and that a function F may be defined with the property that

$$y = F(x_1, \cdots, x_r, \cdots, x_m) = f(x_{11}, \cdots, x_{rk}, \cdots, x_{mn_m}).$$

The functions $x_r = f_r(x_{r1}, \cdots, x_{rk}, \cdots, x_{rn_r})$ are single-valued by construction. The function F would fail to be single-valued only if two different values of y corresponded to a single set of values of $x_1, \cdots, x_m$. Since two vectors $(x'_{r1}, \cdots, x'_{rn_r})$ and $(x''_{r1}, \cdots, x''_{rn_r})$ receive the same number x_r only if they belong to the same element of the rth partition, and belong to the same element of the rth partition only if, given the values of all other elementary variables, they yield the same value of y, it follows that the function F is indeed single-valued.

The proof of Theorem 1 is therefore complete.

4.

Property (a) of the function (2.1) is that $\partial f / \partial x_{rk} > 0$ for all r and k. We found in the course of the proof of Theorem 1 that

$$\frac{\partial f}{\partial x_{rk}} = \frac{\partial F}{\partial x_r} \frac{\partial x_r}{\partial x_{rk}}$$

so that $\partial F / \partial x_r \cdot \partial x_r / \partial x_{rk}$ must be positive. We shall select the functions F and x_r in such a way that both $\partial F / \partial x_r$ and $\partial x_r / \partial x_{rk}$ are always positive; this implies that we shall follow the natural course of maximizing (rather than minimizing) the appropriate function at each stage of the two-stage maximization procedure.

Property (b) of the function (2.1) will be considered at length in Chapter 4 below. We shall find in Chapter 3 that the conditions of Theorem 1 are not alone sufficient for the consistency of two-stage maximization.

CHAPTER 3
Two-Stage Maximization

1.

In this chapter we shall derive the conditions for the consistency of the two-stage maximization procedure described at the beginning of Chapter 2. Certain preliminary mathematical results—Lemmas 2.1 and 2.2 and Theorem 2 and its Corollary—will be needed for the proof of a general result (Theorem 3) on two-stage maximization, and are also needed for the arguments of later chapters. Theorem 2 is due to Leontief (1947a, 1947b) and Nataf (1948), and Theorem 3 to Gorman (1959a) and Strotz (1959).

If, as was mentioned above, we require not only that two-stage maximization be possible, but also that the product of each group quantity-index and price-index equal group expenditure, we need the more special Theorem 4, to be stated and proved in the next chapter.

2.

LEMMA 2.1: *If* $y = f(x_1, x_2, \cdots, x_n)$, *and for each* $r(r = 1, \cdots, n)$, $\partial f/\partial x_r = g_r(x_r)$, *then there exists a set of functions* $F_r(x_r)$ *such that*

$$y = F_1(x_1) + F_2(x_2) + \cdots F_n(x_n).$$

Proof:

$$dy = \sum_{r=1}^{n} \frac{\partial f}{\partial x_r} dx_r = \sum_{r=1}^{n} g_r(x_r)\, dx_r$$

$$\therefore \quad y = \int \sum_{r=1}^{n} g_r(x_r)\, dx_r = \sum_{r=1}^{n} \int g_r(x_r)\, dx_r$$

$$= \sum_{r=1}^{n} h_r(x_r) + k_r = \sum_{r=1}^{n} F_r(x_r).$$

(An additive utility function of the type favoured by Jevons would have the properties set out in Lemma 2.1. The properties of the function described in Lemma 2.2 and Theorem 2, however, correspond to Houthakker's "direct additivity" (Houthakker (1960)), and do not require the assumption of cardinal utility).

LEMMA 2.2: *If* $y = f(x_1, x_2, \cdots, x_n)$ *and for all* $r, s(r, s, = 1, \cdots, m;$ $3 \leqq m \leqq n)$:

$$\frac{\partial f}{\partial x_r} \Big/ \frac{\partial f}{\partial x_s} = \frac{f_r}{f_s} = f_{rs}(x_r, x_s)$$

then there is a set of functions $g_1(x_1), \cdots, g_m(x_m)$ such that for all r, $s = 1, \cdots, m$

$$\frac{f_r}{f_s} = \frac{g_r(x_r)}{g_s(x_s)}$$

Proof: For all r, s and $t = 1, \cdots, m$

$$\frac{f_r}{f_t} = \frac{f_r}{f_s} \div \frac{f_t}{f_s} = \frac{f_{rs}(x_r, x_s)}{f_{ts}(x_t, x_s)}$$

Hence

$$\log\left(\frac{f_r}{f_t}\right) = \log f_{rs}(x_r, x_s) - \log f_{ts}(x_t, x_s)$$

and

$$\frac{\partial^2 \log\left(\frac{f_r}{f_t}\right)}{\partial x_r\, \partial x_t} = 0$$

so that

$$\log\left(\frac{f_r}{f_t}\right) = a_r(x_r) + a_t(x_t) + C$$

$$\therefore \quad \frac{f_r}{f_t} = A_r(x_r) \cdot A_t(x_t).$$

We can therefore eliminate x_s from both numerator and denominator of $f_{rs}(x_r, x_s)/f_{ts}(x_t, x_s)$ to obtain

$$\frac{f_r}{f_t} = \frac{g_r(x_r)}{g_t(x_t)}$$

where $g_r(x_r) = A_r(x_r); \ g_t(x_t) = 1/A_t(x_t)$.

By similar processes, involving in each case the elimination of x_s, we obtain a set of functions $g_i(x_i)(i \neq s)$, with the property that

$$\frac{f_1}{g_1(x_1)} = \cdots = \frac{f_r}{g_r(x_r)} = \frac{f_t}{g_t(x_t)} = \frac{f_u}{g_u(x_u)} = \cdots = \frac{f_m}{g_m(x_m)}.$$

Elimination of x_t would have yielded a set of functions $h_j(x_j)(j \neq t)$ such that

$$\frac{f_1}{h_1(x_1)} = \cdots = \frac{f_r}{h_r(x_r)} = \frac{f_s}{h_s(x_s)} = \frac{f_u}{h_u(x_u)} = \cdots = \frac{f_m}{h_m(x_m)}.$$

Define the variable g_s in such a way that

$$g_s = h_s(x_s)\frac{g_1(x_1)}{h_1(x_1)} = h_s(x_s)\frac{g_2(x_2)}{h_2(x_2)}.^{\dagger}$$

$\dagger$ The second equality holds because $\dfrac{h_s}{h_1} g_1 = \dfrac{f_s}{f_1} g_1 = \dfrac{f_s g_2}{f_2} = \dfrac{h_s g_2}{h_2}.$

18

Since the second expression depends only on x_s and x_1, and the third only on x_s and x_2, it follows that g_s is a function of x_s alone. Moreover, $g_s/g_1 = h_s/h_1 = f_s/f_1$.

The existence of the set of m functions $g_1(x_1), \cdots, g_m(x_m)$ required by the lemma is therefore established.

THEOREM 2: *If* $y = f(x_1, x_2, \cdots, x_n)$ *and for all* $r, s = 1, \cdots, m;$ $3 \leq m \leq n$

$$\frac{f_r}{f_s} = f_{rs}(x_r, x_s)$$

then there exist functions $F_1, F_2, \cdots, F_m$ *and* G *such that*

$$y = G[F_1(x_1) + F_2(x_2) + \cdots + F_m(x_m), x_{m+1}, \cdots, x_n].$$

The theorem postulates a subset of three or more variables, with the property that the marginal rate of substitution between any two variables of the subset depends on the values of those two variables alone. Then that subset of variables can be replaced, in the expression of the function, by a sum of functions; each function in the sum is a function of only one of the variables in the subset.

Proof: Consider first the case where $m = n$. Then by Lemma 2.2 there exist functions $g_r(x_r)(r = 1, \cdots, n)$ such that for all r, s

$$\frac{f_r}{f_s} = \frac{g_r(x_r)}{g_s(x_s)}.$$

Consider a function H such that for each r, $\partial H/\partial x_r = g_r(x_r)$. Then by Lemma 2.1 there is a set of functions $F_1, \cdots, F_n$ such that $H = \sum_{r=1}^{n} F_r(x_r)$.

Now

$$dH = \sum_{r=1}^{n} g_r(x_r)\, dx_r$$

$$dy = \sum_{r=1}^{n} f_r\, dx_r.$$

Since the partial derivatives of the functions H and y are always proportional, it follows that $dH = 0$ when and only when $dy = 0$. Thus any two sets of values of $x_1, \cdots, x_n$ yield equal values of y if and only if they yield equal values of H. Hence y is a function of H, and we may write

$$y = G(H) = G[F_1(x_1) + F_2(x_2) + \cdots + F_n(x_n)].$$

If $3 \leq m < n$, we can find functions $g_1, \cdots, g_m, H$, and $F_1, \cdots, F_m$ exactly as when $m = n$. If the values of $x_{m+1}, \cdots, x_n$ are given, y is a function only of $x_1, \cdots, x_m$ and therefore of H. Hence, as required by the theorem

$$y = G(H, x_{m+1}, \cdots, x_n) = G[F_1(x_1) + F_2(x_2) + \cdots$$

$$+ F_m(x_m), x_{m+1}, \cdots, x_n].$$

COROLLARY TO THEOREM 2: *If* $y = f(x_1, \cdots, x_n)$ *and for all* $r, s = 1,$ $\cdots, n, f_r/f_s = c_{rs} = constant,$ *then* $y = G(a_1x_1 + a_2x_2 + \cdots + a_nx_n + b),$ *where* $a_r/a_s = c_{rs}.$

Proof: The partial derivatives of $H = a_1x_1 + \cdots + a_nx_n + b$ are proportional to those of f, so that y is a function of H.

3.

In proving the general theorem on two-stage maximization (Theorem 3), it will be convenient to write the "ungrouped" function (2.1)

$$y = f(x_{11}, \cdots, x_{1n_1}, \cdots, x_{r1}, \cdots, x_{rn_r}, \cdots, x_{m1}, \cdots, x_{mn_m})$$

in "indirect" form. For this purpose, utility or output is regarded not as a function of commodities or inputs, but as the maximum utility or output obtainable with a given expenditure E at prices $p_{11}, \cdots, p_{mn_m}$

$$y = \phi(E, p_{11}, \cdots, p_{1n_1}, \cdots, p_{rk}, \cdots, p_{m1}, \cdots, p_{mn_m}).$$

If the elementary variables are to be grouped, it is necessary first that the "weak separability" conditions of Theorem 1 be satisfied, so that a set of quantity indices $x_r(x_{r1}, \cdots, x_{rn_r})$ exist. Each quantity index may be thought of as representing the utility or output derived from a group of commodities or inputs, and may also be written in indirect form, as a function of expenditure on that group, E_r, and the prices of members of that group. If the two-stage maximization procedure is to be consistent, there must exist a set of price-indices, $P_1, \cdots, P_m$, where $P_r = P_r$ $(p_{r1}, \cdots, p_{rn_r})$, such that group expenditure E_r is a function only of total expenditure E and the values of the price-indices.

Formally, consistent two-stage maximization implies that we can write

$$y = \psi(\phi_1, \phi_2, \cdots, \phi_m) \tag{3.1}$$

where for all $r = 1, \cdots, m$

$$\phi_r = \phi_r[E_r(E, P_1, \cdots, P_m), p_{r1}, \cdots, p_{rn_r}] \tag{3.2}$$

and

$$E = \sum_{r=1}^{m} E_r. \tag{3.3}$$

Now if there are only two groups of commodities, the "weak separability" conditions of Theorem 1 are sufficient. We need to show that price-indices P_1 and P_2 exist so that

$$E_1 = E_1(E, P_1, P_2) \quad \text{and} \quad E_2 = E_2(E, P_1, P_2).$$

The marginal rate of substitution between two commodities in (say) the first group depends, by weak separability, only on the quantities of the first group. Hence, if the prices of the first group remain unchanged, a change in the price of a member of the second group can affect the quantities of the first group only by changing expenditure on the first group, E_1. And any two changes in the prices of the second group which have the same effect on E_1 will have the same effect on the first group quantities.

Let us then define a price-index $P_2(p_{21}, \cdots, p_{2n_2})$ in such a way that for all $h, i = 1, \cdots, n_1; j, k = 1, \cdots, n_2$

$$\frac{\dfrac{\partial x_{1h}}{\partial p_{2j}}}{\dfrac{\partial x_{1h}}{\partial p_{2k}}} = \frac{\dfrac{\partial x_{1i}}{\partial p_{2j}}}{\dfrac{\partial x_{1i}}{\partial p_{2k}}} = \frac{\dfrac{\partial x_{1h}}{\partial E_1}\dfrac{\partial E_1}{\partial p_{2j}}}{\dfrac{\partial x_{1h}}{\partial E_1}\dfrac{\partial E_1}{\partial p_{2k}}} = \frac{\dfrac{\partial x_{1i}}{\partial E_1}\dfrac{\partial E_1}{\partial p_{2j}}}{\dfrac{\partial x_{1i}}{\partial E_1}\dfrac{\partial E_1}{\partial p_{2k}}} = \frac{\dfrac{\partial E_1}{\partial p_{2j}}}{\dfrac{\partial E_1}{\partial p_{2k}}} = \frac{\dfrac{\partial P_2}{\partial p_{2j}}}{\dfrac{\partial P_2}{\partial p_{2k}}}$$

An index $P_1(p_{11}, \cdots, p_{1n_1})$ can be similarly defined so that

$$\frac{\dfrac{\partial x_{2j}}{\partial p_{1h}}}{\dfrac{\partial x_{2j}}{\partial p_{1i}}} = \frac{\dfrac{\partial E_2}{\partial p_{1h}}}{\dfrac{\partial E_2}{\partial p_{1i}}} = \frac{\dfrac{\partial P_1}{\partial p_{1h}}}{\dfrac{\partial P_1}{\partial p_{1i}}}$$

The index P_2 as defined belongs to the function $E_1(E, P_1, P_2)$ and the index P_1 to the function $E_2(E, P_1, P_2)$. We must also show that the indices P_1 and P_2 can be entered in the functions $E_1(\ )$ and $E_2(\ )$ respectively. This is so, since with only two groups $E_1 + E_2 = E$, so that $\partial E_1/\partial p_{2j} + \partial E_2/\partial p_{2j} = 0$, etc., and therefore

$$\frac{\dfrac{\partial E_1}{\partial p_{2j}}}{\dfrac{\partial E_1}{\partial p_{2k}}} = \frac{\dfrac{\partial E_2}{\partial p_{2j}}}{\dfrac{\partial E_2}{\partial p_{2k}}} = \frac{\dfrac{\partial P_2}{\partial p_{2j}}}{\dfrac{\partial P_2}{\partial p_{2k}}} \quad \text{and} \quad \frac{\dfrac{\partial E_2}{\partial p_{1h}}}{\dfrac{\partial E_2}{\partial p_{1i}}} = \frac{\dfrac{\partial E_1}{\partial p_{1h}}}{\dfrac{\partial E_1}{\partial p_{1i}}} = \frac{\dfrac{\partial P_1}{\partial p_{1h}}}{\dfrac{\partial P_1}{\partial p_{1i}}}.$$

4.

If there are more than two groups, however, weak separability is not sufficient, as Theorem 3 shows.

THEOREM 3: *The utility or production function may be written in the form* (3.1), *where each* ϕ_r *can be expressed in the form* (3.2), *only if the* "*weak separability*" *conditions of Theorem 1 are satisfied and:*

either (i) *there are only two groups;*

or (ii) *each group quantity index can be written in direct form as a homogeneous function of the quantities in the group;*

or (iii) *the quantity indices for all groups but one* (*say the first*) *are homogeneous, and* y *may be written as*

$$y = \psi[\phi_1, H(\phi_2, \cdots, \phi_m)] \tag{3.4}$$

or (iv) *the quantity indices for all groups beyond the* d^{th} *are homogeneous, and* y *may be written in the following additive form:*

$$y = \psi\left[\sum_{r=1}^{d} G_r(\phi_r) + H(\phi_{d+1}, \cdots, \phi_m)\right] \tag{3.5}$$

Note that case (iv) implies that the marginal rate of substitution between any two elementary variables in any two *distinct* "non-homogeneous" groups (groups 1 to d) must be independent of the value of any elementary variable in any third group. We can show this by pointing out that if the qth and r^{th} groups are both non-homogeneous, it follows from (3.5) that

$$\frac{\frac{\partial y}{\partial x_{qj}}}{\frac{\partial y}{\partial x_{rk}}} = \frac{\psi' \frac{\partial G_q}{\partial \phi_q} \frac{\partial \phi_q}{\partial x_{qj}}}{\psi' \frac{\partial G_r}{\partial \phi_r} \frac{\partial \phi_r}{\partial x_{rk}}}$$

which is a function only of $x_{q1}, \cdots, x_{qn_q}, x_{r1}, \cdots, x_{rn_r}$.

This is clearly a more stringent condition than that of Theorem 1, and has been termed "strong separability" by Gorman (1959a) and Strotz (1959).

The proof of Theorem 3 is lengthy, and we shall confine ourselves to an outline, referring the reader to the papers by Gorman and Strotz for the details.

Proof of Theorem 3: Maximization of (3.1) subject to (3.3) yields the conditions that for all q and $r = 1, \cdots, m$

$$\psi_q \frac{\partial \phi_q}{\partial E_q} = \psi_r \frac{\partial \phi_r}{\partial E_r} \tag{3.6}$$

If we differentiate (3.6) with respect to the prices p_{sj} and p_{sk} ($s \neq q, r$) a little manipulation yields

$$(\psi_{sq}\psi_r - \psi_{sr}\psi_q) \begin{vmatrix} \dfrac{\partial \phi_s}{\partial p_{sj}} & \dfrac{\partial \phi_s}{\partial p_{sk}} \\ \dfrac{\partial P_s}{\partial p_{sj}} & \dfrac{\partial P_s}{\partial p_{sk}} \end{vmatrix} = 0 \tag{3.7}$$

where of course $\psi_q = \partial\psi/\partial\phi_a$, $\psi_{sq} = \partial^2\psi/\partial\phi_s\partial\phi_q$. Therefore one of the two parentheses of (3.7) must vanish.

Part (ii) of Theorem 3 corresponds to the case where the second parenthesis vanishes for all s. It may be shown that for all s, j, and k,

$$\frac{\dfrac{\partial\psi}{\partial p_{sj}}}{\dfrac{\partial\psi}{\partial p_{sk}}} = \frac{\dfrac{\partial\phi_s}{\partial p_{sj}}}{\dfrac{\partial\phi_s}{\partial p_{sk}}} = \frac{\dfrac{\partial P_s}{\partial p_{sj}}}{\dfrac{\partial P_s}{\partial p_{sk}}}.$$

Thus the marginal rate of substitution between any two *prices* of the sth group, which, by the conditions for a maximum of the indirect utility function is equal to the ratio of the corresponding *quantities*, is equal to $(\partial P_s/\partial p_{sj})/(\partial P_s/\partial p_{sk})$, which depends only on the prices $p_{s1}, \cdots, p_{sn_s}$. But if the ratio of any two quantities in the sth group depends only on the prices of the sth group, and is therefore independent of E_s, the Engel curves for the group are straight lines through the origin. Hence ϕ_s can be written in direct form as a homogeneous function of $x_{s1}, \cdots, x_{sn_s}$.

If the second parenthesis of (3.7) vanishes for $s = 2, \cdots, m$, but not for $s = 1$, it follows that

$$\psi_{1r}\psi_q - \psi_{1q}\psi_r = 0$$

for all q, $r \neq 1$. Application of Theorem 1 leads directly to equation (3.4). This corresponds to part (iii) of Theorem 3.

Part (iv) of Theorem 3 is the case where the second parenthesis of (3.7) fails to vanish for more than one group. Let us denote these non-homogeneous groups by $a = 1, \cdots, d$, and the homogeneous groups by q, $r = d + 1, \cdots, m$.[2] We then have, for all a, q, r

$$\psi_{aq}\psi_r - \psi_{ar}\psi_q = 0.$$

Application of Theorem 1 leads directly to

$$y = \psi[\phi_1, \phi_2, \cdots, \phi_d, H(\phi_{d+1}, \cdots, \phi_m)] \tag{3.8}$$

If we can now show: (1) that the marginal rate of substitution between any $\phi_a(a = 1, \cdots, d)$ and H depends only on the values of ϕ_a and H; (2) that the marginal rate of substitution between any ϕ_a and ϕ_b (a, $b = 1, \cdots, d$) depends only on the values of ϕ_a and ϕ_b, direct application of Theorem 2 will enable us to write (3.8) as (3.5).

The result (1) is obtained by taking a, b as any two non-homogeneous groups and r as any homogeneous group, and showing that if, as is required by (3.7), $\psi_{ab}\psi_r - \psi_{ar}\psi_b = 0$, then $\psi_b\psi_{aH} - \psi_H\psi_{ba} = 0$. The

---

[2] The argument is considerably simplified if there is only one homogeneous group.

result (2) is obtained by again taking a, b as any two non-homogeneous groups, and r as any other group, whether homogeneous or not. It is then necessary only to observe that since $\psi_{ab}\psi_r - \psi_{ar}\psi_b = 0$ and $\psi_{ba}\psi_r - \psi_{br}\psi_a = 0$, it follows that $\psi_{ar}\psi_b - \psi_{br}\psi_a = 0$. In the case of both (1) and (2), Theorem 1 leads directly to the conclusion desired.

CHAPTER 4
Homogeneous Functional Separability

1.

We shall now state and prove a theorem which embodies the requirement, stated in Chapter 2 above, that the product of each group's quantity index and its price index must equal expenditure on the group. We argued earlier that this condition is necessary if quantity indices are to be treated in all respects as if they were quantities of elementary commodities or inputs.

THEOREM 4: *The necessary and sufficient conditions for both (a) the consistency of the two-stage maximization procedure, and (b) the existence for each group of a quantity-index x_r and a price-index P_r such that group expenditure $E_r = P_r x_r (r = 1, \cdots, m)$, are that each quantity-index be a function homogeneous of degree one in its elementary commodities or inputs.*

Proof: Let

$$x_r = f_r(x_{r1}, \cdots, x_{rn_r})$$

$$P_r = P_r(p_{r1}, \cdots, p_{rn_r})$$

$$E_r = P_r x_r = \sum_{k=1}^{n_r} p_{rk} x_{rk}.$$

If each x_{rk} is changed in the same proportion α, with each p_{rk} held constant, then $E_r = P_r x_r$ must change in the proportion α. But with each p_{rk} constant, P_r does not change. Hence x_r must change in the proportion α, and f_r is homogeneous of degree one. This property of the function f_r is therefore necessary for part (b) of the theorem.

But is this property sufficient to ensure the existence of a price-index P_r such that $P_r x_r = E_r$? To show that it is so, let us define P_r as E_r/x_r and show that P_r is a function of the prices $p_{r1}, \cdots, p_{rn_r}$ alone. Take any given set of prices, and change E_r in the proportion α. Since the function f_r is homogeneous, the group Engel curves or expansion paths are straight lines through the origin,[1] so that each x_{rk}, and therefore also x_r, will change in the proportion α. P_r therefore does not change, and is a function of $p_{r1}, \cdots, p_{rn_r}$. The argument of the first paragraph of this proof will show, *mutatis mutandis*, that the function P_r is also homogeneous of degree one.

---

[1] This statement implies that the group iso-product surfaces or indifference surfaces are smoothly convex to the origin. Theorem 6 below shows that this is so if the ungrouped function (2.1) satisfies the Hicksian stability conditions (see above, pp. 10–11).

It remains to be shown that, if each quantity index is homogeneous of degree one (we shall call this property the "homogeneous functional separability" of the utility or production function), then the two-stage maximization procedure is consistent.

In the first stage, $y = F(x_1, \cdots, x_m)$ is maximized subject to $\sum_{r=1}^{m} P_r x_r = E$. This yields, for all $q, r = 1, \cdots, m$

$$\frac{\dfrac{\partial y}{\partial x_q}}{\dfrac{\partial y}{\partial x_r}} = \frac{P_q}{P_r}.$$

In the second stage, $x_r = x_r(x_{r1}, \cdots, x_{rn_r})$ is maximized subject to $\sum_{k=1}^{n_r} p_{rk} x_{rk} = E_r$. This yields, for all $j, k = 1, \cdots, n_r$

$$\frac{\dfrac{\partial x_r}{\partial x_{rj}}}{\dfrac{\partial x_r}{\partial x_{rk}}} = \frac{p_{rj}}{p_{rk}}.$$

We wish to be satisfied that for all q, r, j, k

$$\frac{\dfrac{\partial y}{\partial x_{qj}}}{\dfrac{\partial y}{\partial x_{rk}}} = \frac{p_{qj}}{p_{rk}}.$$

This causes no difficulty if $q = r$, since

$$\frac{\dfrac{\partial y}{\partial x_{qj}}}{\dfrac{\partial y}{\partial x_{qk}}} = \frac{\dfrac{\partial y}{\partial x_q}\dfrac{\partial x_q}{\partial x_{qj}}}{\dfrac{\partial y}{\partial x_q}\dfrac{\partial x_q}{\partial x_{qk}}} = \frac{\dfrac{\partial x_q}{\partial x_{qj}}}{\dfrac{\partial x_q}{\partial x_{qk}}} = \frac{p_{qj}}{p_{qk}}.$$

But if $q \neq r$

$$\frac{\dfrac{\partial y}{\partial x_{qj}}}{\dfrac{\partial y}{\partial x_{rk}}} = \frac{\dfrac{\partial y}{\partial x_q}\dfrac{\partial x_q}{\partial x_{qj}}}{\dfrac{\partial y}{\partial x_r}\dfrac{\partial x_r}{\partial x_{rk}}} = \frac{P_q\dfrac{\partial x_q}{\partial x_{qj}}}{P_r\dfrac{\partial x_r}{\partial x_{rk}}}.$$

If $P_q(\partial x_q/\partial x_{qj}) = p_{qj}$, $P_r(\partial x_r/\partial x_{rk}) = p_{rk}$, our requirements are satisfied. This will now be shown.

The necessary conditions for maximization of x_r subject to

$$\sum_{k=1}^{n_r} p_{rz} x_{rk} = E_r$$

are that for all $k = 1, \cdots, n_r$

$$\frac{\partial x_r}{\partial x_{rk}} = \lambda p_{rk} \qquad (4.1)$$

where λ is a Lagrange multiplier. If we multiply each equation (4.1) by the appropriate x_{rk} and add, we obtain

$$\sum_{k=1}^{n_r} x_{rk} \frac{\partial x_r}{\partial x_{rk}} = \lambda \sum_{k=1}^{n_r} p_{rk} x_{rk} = \lambda E_r = \lambda P_r x_r.$$

But since x_r is homogeneous of degree one in the x_{rk}'s, we have by Euler's theorem

$$x_r = \lambda P_r x_r, \quad \text{whence} \quad \lambda = \frac{1}{P_r}.$$

It follows from (4.1) that $P_r \ (\partial x_r / \partial x_{rk}) = p_{rk}$, as required.

2.

Let us illustrate Theorem 4 by an example. Suppose that the over-all utility or production function is of the Cobb-Douglas variety

$$y = \prod_{r=1}^{m} \prod_{k=1}^{n_r} x_{rk}^{a_{rk}}.$$

This may be written as

$$y = \prod_{r=1}^{m} \left(\prod_{k=1}^{n_r} x_{rk}^{a_{rk}/\sum_k a_{rk}} \right)^{\sum_{k=1}^{n_r} a_{rk}}$$

If we write $a_{rk} / \sum_k a_{rk}$ as b_{rk}, then of course $\sum_k b_{rk} = 1$. Then $x_r = \prod_{k=1}^{n_r} x_{rk}^{b_{rk}}$ meets the conditions of Theorem 4.

The corresponding price-index P_r is obtained as follows. It is well-known that with a utility or production function of this type, the proportion of E_r devoted to the purchase of x_{rk} is equal to b_{rk}. Hence

$$P_r x_r = \frac{p_{rk} x_{rk}}{b_{rk}} = \prod_{k=1}^{n_r} \left(\frac{p_{rk} x_{rk}}{b_{rk}} \right)^{b_{rk}} = \prod_{k=1}^{n_r} x_{rk}^{b_{rk}} \prod_{k=1}^{n_r} \left(\frac{p_{rk}}{b_{rk}} \right)^{b_{rk}}$$

since $\sum_k b_{rk} = 1$. It follows that

$$P_r = \prod_{k=1}^{n_r} \left(\frac{p_{rk}}{b_{rk}} \right)^{b_{rk}}.$$

The appropriate quantity-index is a weighted geometric mean of quantities, where the weights are the constant expenditure proportions; the price-index is a similarly weighted geometric mean of prices, each divided by the corresponding expenditure proportion.

3.

The restrictions on the utility or production function which have been found to be necessary for the type of grouping of variables discussed in this chapter are stringent. They are necessary, however, only if we seek our conditions in the form of the function alone. It may well be (and this is a recurrent theme throughout this volume) that aggregation is made consistent because of restrictions on the behavior of "independent" variables.

Suppose, for example, that there is a group of commodities that must always be purchased in fixed proportions (cf. Leontief (1936)). The group price-index will be the total price of a bundle of the commodities in the given proportions, and the quantity index the number of such bundles. Clearly this group of commodities can be treated in all respects as if it were a single commodity.

If, on the other hand, the *prices* of a group of commodities or inputs always move in the same proportion, any number proportional to any one price will serve as the group price-index, and the quantity index may be defined as expenditure on the group divided by the price-index. Such a quantity-index will be homogeneous of degree one in the elementary variables. The group Engel curves and expansion paths will not necessarily be straight lines through the origin, but this property was used in the proof of Theorem 4 only to establish that P_r was a function of $p_{r1}, \cdots, p_{rn_r}$; this is plainly so in the present case.

Hicks says: "a collection of physical things can always be treated as if they were divisible into units of a single commodity so long as their relative prices can be assumed to remain unchanged, in the particular problem in hand." (Hicks (1946), p. 33). The argument of this chapter suggests that the general condition for such treatment of a group of commodities is the possibility of defining a group quantity-index that is homogeneous of degree one; price-proportionality is a special case of this. (Quantity-proportionality might be regarded as a degenerate case of the same condition).

4.

We have been concerned so far with the circumstances in which the satisfaction of the first-order conditions for a maximum of utility or output at each stage of the two-stage budgeting procedure ensures the satisfaction of the first-order conditions for a maximum of the un-grouped function $y = f(x_{11}, \cdots, x_{mn_m})$. Since we have said nothing about second-order conditions, it may be argued that we have not yet completed the proof of the proposition, stated in Theorem 4, that homogeneous functional separability makes the two-stage budgeting procedure consistent, in the sense that the quantities x_{rk} resulting from the single-stage and the two-stage procedures are identical.

We shall now complete the argument by showing that if the function $y = f(x_{11}, \cdots, x_{mn_m})$ satisfies the Hicksian stability conditions, homogeneous functional separability ensures that the second-order conditions are satisfied at each stage of the two-stage maximization procedure. First we shall show, in Theorem 5, that if the function $y = f(x_{11}, \cdots, x_{mn_m})$ satisfies the Hicksian stability conditions, the same is true of the grouped utility or production function $F(x_1, \cdots, x_m)$. Theorem 5 is based on a proof attributed to Samuelson by Solow (1956b, p. 104n.).

It is intuitively obvious that the Hicksian stability conditions—that is, the alternation in sign of the principal minors of the determinant (2.3) described on page 10 above, which we have sometimes equated with the smooth convexity to the origin of iso-product surfaces or indifference surfaces—are equivalent to the following: If (x') and (x'') are any two distinct points on the same indifference surface or iso-product surface, then the mid-point of the straight line joining (x') and (x'') yields a higher value of y than either (x') or (x''). This assertion may be stated formally as a lemma.

LEMMA 5.1. *The Hicksian stability conditions on the function* (2.1) *are equivalent to the condition that, for any two vectors* $(x') = (x'_{11}, \cdots, x'_{rk}, \cdots, x'_{mn_m})$ *and* $(x'') = (x''_{11}, \cdots, x''_{rk}, \cdots, x''_{mn_m})$ *such that* $f(x') = f(x'')$ *and* $(x') \neq (x'')$,

$$f(x') = f(x'') < f\left(\frac{x' + x''}{2}\right)$$

where

$$\left(\frac{x' + x''}{2}\right) = \left(\frac{x'_{11} + x''_{11}}{2}, \cdots, \frac{x'_{rk} + x''_{rk}}{2}, \cdots, \frac{x'_{mn_m} + x''_{mn_m}}{2}\right).$$

THEOREM 5: *If it is possible to write the function* (2.1):

$$y = f(x_{11}, \cdots, x_{rk}, \cdots, x_{mn_m})$$

in the form (2.4):

$$y = F(x_1, \cdots, x_r, \cdots, x_m)$$

with each x_r ($r = 1, \cdots, m$) *homogeneous of degree one in* $x_{r1}, \cdots, x_{rn_r}$, *and if the function* f *satisfies the Hicksian stability conditions, then the function* F *satisfies the Hicksian stability conditions.*

Proof: We proceed by grouping one set of variables at a time. Consider therefore the function F_1, where

$$y = F_1(x_1, x_{21}, \cdots, x_{mn_m}) = f(x_{11}, \cdots, x_{1n_1}, x_{21}, \cdots, x_{mn_m})$$

and $x_1 = x_1(x_{11}, \cdots, x_{1n_1})$ is homogeneous of degree one.

Let $x_1' = x_1(x_{11}', \cdots, x_{1n_1}')$ and $x_1'' = x_1(x_{11}'', \cdots, x_{1n_1}'')$, where for each $k = 1, \cdots, n_1$, $x_{1k}'' = \alpha x_{1k}'$, and $0 \leq \alpha \neq 1$. Then $x_1'' = \alpha x_1'$.

Consider two sets of values of variables in groups other than the first, $x_{21}', \cdots, x_{mn_m}'$ and $x_{21}'', \cdots, x_{mn_m}''$, such that

$$f(x_{11}', \cdots, x_{1n_1}', x_{21}', \cdots, x_{mn_m}') = f(x_{11}'', \cdots, x_{1n_1}'', x_{21}'', \cdots, x_{mn_m}'').$$

It follows from Lemma 5.1, together with the hypotheses that the function f satisfies the Hicksian stability conditions and that the function x_1 is homogeneous of degree one, that:

$$F_1(x_1', x_{21}', \cdots, x_{mn_m}') = F_1(x_1'', x_{21}'', \cdots, x_{mn_m}'')$$

$$= f(x_{11}', \cdots, x_{1n_1}', x_{21}', \cdots, x_{mn_m}') = f(x_{11}'', \cdots, x_{1n_1}'', x_{21}'', \cdots, x_{mn_m}'')$$

$$< f\left(\frac{x_{11}' + x_{11}''}{2}, \cdots, \frac{x_{1n_1}' + x_{1n_1}''}{2}, \frac{x_{21}' + x_{21}''}{2}, \cdots, \frac{x_{mn_m}' + x_{mn_m}''}{2}\right)$$

$$= F_1\left[x_1\left(\frac{x_{11}' + x_{11}''}{2}, \cdots, \frac{x_{1n_1}' + x_{1n_1}''}{2}\right), \frac{x_{21}' + x_{21}''}{2}, \cdots, \frac{x_{mn_m}' + x_{mn_m}''}{2}\right]$$

$$= F_1\left[x_1\left(x_{11}'\left(\frac{1+\alpha}{2}\right), \cdots, x_{1n_1}'\left(\frac{1+\alpha}{2}\right)\right), \frac{x_{21}' + x_{21}''}{2}, \cdots, \frac{x_{mn_m}' + x_{mn_m}''}{2}\right]$$

$$= F_1\left[x_1'\left(\frac{1+\alpha}{2}\right), \frac{x_{21}' + x_{21}''}{2}, \cdots, \frac{x_{mn_m}' + x_{mn_m}''}{2}\right]$$

$$= F_1\left(\frac{x_1' + x_1''}{2}, \frac{x_{21}' + x_{21}''}{2}, \cdots, \frac{x_{mn_m}' + x_{mn_m}''}{2}\right).$$

It now follows from Lemma 5.1 that the function F_1 satisfies the Hicksian stability conditions. The proof is completed by grouping a second set of variables in the function F_1 and carrying out the same argument, continuing until the function $F(x_1, \cdots, x_r, \cdots, x_m)$ is reached.

5.

Theorem 5 implies that the satisfaction of the first-order conditions for a maximum of $F(x_1, \cdots, x_r, \cdots, x_m)$ subject to $\sum_{r=1}^{m} P_r x_r = E$ is sufficient to ensure that a maximum of y is attained. It can now be shown quite easily that the choice, for each r, of the quantities $x_{r1}, \cdots, x_{rn_r}$, subject to $\sum_{k=1}^{n_r} p_{rk} x_{rk} = E_r = P_r x_r$, yields a maximum of y. We may consider three sets of circumstances in which two-stage maximization is consistent, and in which functions $P_r(p_{r1}, \cdots, p_{rn_r})$ and $x_r(x_{r1}, \cdots, x_{rn_r})$ exist such that $P_r x_r = E_r$. In the first case, the justification for the grouping of variables is found in the form of the function $f(x_{11}, \cdots, x_{mn_m})$. In the second case, the prices of a group of commodities or inputs always move proportionally, while in the third case the quantities in a group always move proportionally.

The case of quantity-proportionality, described earlier as degenerate, is one to which the proof of Theorem 5 can not be applied. Each group indifference surface or equal-product surface consists of a single point, and the Hicksian stability conditions do not hold among members of the group. The Hicksian conditions must be taken to apply to the relationships between the number of bundles, of fixed composition, of commodities or inputs in the group, and the number of units of other commodities; this amounts to assuming Theorem 5 directly.

In the other two cases, where separability depends on the form of the function f or on price-proportionality in the group, we may, if we choose, regard the selection of the quantities $x_{r1}, \cdots, x_{rn_r}$ as resulting from the maximization of a function of these quantities subject to $\sum_{k=1}^{n_r} p_{rk}x_{rk} = E_r$. In either of the two cases, the result will satisfy the second-order conditions for a maximum of $f(x_{11}, \cdots, x_{mn_m})$, since in the final equilibrium, with the quantities in all other groups given, the function of $x_{r1}, \cdots, x_{rn_r}$ maximized is in effect $f(\overline{x_{11}}, \cdots, \overline{x_{qn_q}}, x_{r1}, \cdots, x_{rn_r}, \overline{x_{s1}}, \cdots, \overline{x_{mn_m}})$, which plainly satisfies the Hicksian stability conditions if the function (2.1) does so.

The difference between the two cases is that when the separability of a group is based on price-proportionality, there is no reason to suppose that in the *absence* of price-proportionality the group would be even weakly separable. Hence the equal-product surfaces or indifference surfaces relating to $x_{r1}, \cdots, x_{rn_r}$ in the function $f(\overline{x_{11}}, \cdots, \overline{x_{qn_q}}, x_{r1}, \cdots, x_{rn_r}, \overline{x_{s1}}, \cdots, \overline{x_{mn_m}})$ will in general be different for different values of the variables in groups other than the rth.

When separability depends on the form of the function f, on the other hand, there is a function $x_r(x_{r1}, \cdots, x_{rn_r})$ whose equal-product or indifference surfaces do not change with changes in the values of variables in other groups. The argument of the preceding paragraph can of course be applied. But an alternative method of establishing the consistency of two-stage maximization is available in this case: it can be shown that the functions $x_r(x_{r1}, \cdots, x_{rn_r})$ themselves obey the Hicksian stability conditions. The proof of this theorem (cf. Solow, *loc. cit.,*) which depends only on weak separability, completes the argument of this chapter.

THEOREM 6: *If it is possible to write the function (2.1) in the form (2.4), with $\partial F/\partial x_r > 0$ for each r, and if the function (2.1) satisfies the Hicksian stability conditions, then each of the functions $x_r(x_{r1}, \cdots, x_{rn_r})$ satisfies the Hicksian stability conditions.*

Proof: Consider again the function F_1:

$$y = F_1(x_1, x_{21}, \cdots, x_{mn_m}) = f(x_{11}, \cdots, x_{1n_1}, x_{21}, \cdots, x_{mn_m}).$$

For any two distinct vectors $x'_{11}, \cdots, x'_{1n_1}$ and $x''_{11}, \cdots, x''_{1n_1}$ such that $x_1(x'_{11}, \cdots, x'_{1n_1}) = x_1(x''_{11}, \cdots, x''_{1n_1}) = x^*_1$, and for any set of values $x'_{21}, \cdots, x'_{mn_m}$, we have:

$$F_1(x^*_1, x'_{21}, \cdots, x'_{mn_m})$$

$$= f(x'_{11}, \cdots, x'_{1n_1}, x'_{21}, \cdots, x'_{mn_m}) = f(x''_{11}, \cdots, x''_{1n_1}, x'_{21}, \cdots, x'_{mn_m})$$

$$< f\left(\frac{x'_{11} + x''_{11}}{2}, \cdots, \frac{x'_{1n_1} + x''_{1n_1}}{2}, \frac{x'_{21} + x'_{21}}{2}, \cdots, \frac{x'_{mn_m} + x'_{mn_m}}{2}\right)$$

$$= F_1\left[x_1\left(\frac{x'_{11} + x''_{11}}{2}, \cdots, \frac{x'_{1n_1} + x''_{1n_1}}{2}\right), x'_{21}, \cdots, x'_{mn_m}\right].$$

By virtue of the assumption (see p. 15 above) that in a function like F_1 in which variables are grouped, $\partial F_1/\partial x_1 > 0$, it follows that

$$x_1\left(\frac{x'_{11} + x''_{11}}{2}, \cdots, \frac{x'_{1n_1} + x''_{1n_1}}{2}\right) > x^*_1 = x_1(x'_{11}, \cdots, x'_{1n_1})$$

$$= x_1(x''_{11}, \cdots, x''_{1n_1}).$$

The theorem then follows by Lemma 5.1.

6.

We have found in Part II that if groups of commodities are to be treated as single commodities, an indispensable condition is the property of "weak separability" discussed in Chapter 2. But it was shown in Chapter 3 that if a common budgeting procedure—that of first allocating expenditure between groups of goods (e.g. food, clothing, entertainment, etc.) and then within groups—is to be satisfactory, and if we wish to distinguish more than two groups, then either "strong separability" or "homogeneous separability" is necessary.

We have argued in Chapter 4 that if we are to treat groups of goods in all respects as if they were single goods, we must require homogeneous separability. This condition may come about not only through the properties of the utility or production function itself, but also because the quantities or prices of members of a group move proportionally. Homogeneous separability was also found to ensure that the second-order conditions for a maximum are satisfied by the two-stage budgeting procedure.

Applications of the concept of functional separability are to be found in papers by Koopmans (1960), who analyzes time-preference in terms of it, by Pearce (1961), who employs it to free Frisch's methods of estimating demand-elasticities from dependence on cardinal utility, and by Gorman (1963), who examines the separability of variables in the additive logarithmic demand functions of Houthakker and Arrow. See also the references given in Morishima's brief survey (1961).

Part III
AGGREGATION OF ECONOMIC RELATIONS

CHAPTER 5

Degrees of Freedom at a Maximum: the Importance of Linearity

1.

In part III we shall be concerned not with the grouping of variables in a single function, but with the aggregation problems raised by the presence of a number of different functions. The reader may think, for the time being, of the independent variables to be introduced in this chapter as the "elementary" variables of Part II. (cf. below, pp. 53–54).

We assume the existence of a number of individual functions or "micro-relations"—for example, household consumption as a function of its income and other variables, individual utility as a function of commodities consumed, firm or industry output as a function of inputs. We seek the conditions in which an aggregate of the individual dependent variables—aggregate consumption, "social utility," industry output or national output—can be expressed consistently as a function of aggregates of the independent variables—aggregates of incomes and other variables, aggregates of commodities or inputs.

Consistency means that a knowledge of the "macro-relation" (the function relating the aggregates), and of the values of the aggregate independent variables, would lead to the same value of the aggregate dependent variable as a knowledge of the micro-relations and of the values of the individual independent variables.[1]

Formally, we consider a set of n individual functions $(s = 1, \cdots, n)$

$$y_s = f_s(x_{1s}, \cdots, x_{rs}, \cdots, x_{ms}). \tag{5.1}$$

We assume that $x_{rs} \geqq 0$, but since the functions f_s are not necessarily utility or production functions, we do not in general assume that they have properties (a) and (b) of the function (2.1) (see above, p. 10)[2].

We wish to be able to write

$$y = F(x_1, \cdots, x_m) \tag{5.2}$$

where y and $x_1, \cdots, x_m$ are defined by the aggregating functions:

$$y = y(y_1, \cdots, y_s, \cdots, y_n) \tag{5.3}$$

$$x_r = x_r(x_{r1}, \cdots, x_{rs}, \cdots, x_{rn})(r = 1, \cdots, m) \tag{5.4}$$

---

[1] We are, in other words, concerned with what Malinvaud (1956a) terms problems of prediction rather than problems of decision.

[2] A more general function than (5.1) could have been used; see, for example, Theil (1954), p. 29. The functions (5.1) are, however, general enough for most aggregation problems (but see below, p. 42).

2.

We shall find it very useful to follow May (1946, 1947) in laying stress on the importance of the number of degrees of freedom enjoyed by the "independent" variables. We have already discovered in Chapter 4 that a limitation of these degrees of freedom (proportionality of the quantities or prices of a group of commodities or inputs) can facilitate aggregation; such limitations will be considered in later chapters. In this chapter, however, we shall assume that there are no restrictions on the values taken by the variables x_{rs} (apart from their non-negativity), so that the number of degrees of freedom is mn.

The first important theorem, on which many of our subsequent results depend, is little more than an application of remarks made in Chapter 1.

THEOREM 7: *Necessary conditions for the functions* (5.1) *to be aggregated to the function* (5.2), *when the variables* x_{rs} *are free to take on all values, are that, for all* $r = 1, \cdots , m$ *and* $s = 1, \cdots , n$

$$\frac{\partial F}{\partial x_r} \frac{\partial x_r}{\partial x_{rs}} = \frac{\partial y}{\partial y_s} \frac{\partial f_s}{\partial x_{rs}}. \tag{5.5}$$

Proof: We must have

$$dy = \sum_{r=1}^{m} \frac{\partial F}{\partial x_r} dx_r = \sum_{r=1}^{m} \sum_{s=1}^{n} \frac{\partial F}{\partial x_r} \frac{\partial x_r}{\partial x_{rs}} dx_{rs}$$

and

$$dy = \sum_{s=1}^{n} \frac{\partial y}{\partial y_s} dy_s = \sum_{r=1}^{m} \sum_{s=1}^{n} \frac{\partial y}{\partial y_s} \frac{\partial f_s}{\partial x_{rs}} dx_{rs}.$$

Since the variables can take on any values, the coefficients of dx_{rs} in the two expressions for dy must be equal for each pair of values of r and s. This is what the theorem states.

3.

The following theorem is due to Nataf (1948), and constitutes his answer to a problem posed by Klein (1946a). It shows the remarkable importance, in aggregation problems, of the linearity of the functions involved, be they micro-relations, macro-relations, or functions defining aggregates. Illustrations of the theorem will be given later in the chapter.

THEOREM 8: *Necessary and sufficient conditions for the aggregation of the functions* (5.1) *to the function* (5.2), *when the variables* x_{rs} *are free to take on all values, are that there exist functions* $G, H, g_r, h_s, G_r, H_s,$ g_{rs}, h_{rs} *such that*

$$y = H[h_1(y_1) + \cdots + h_n(y_n)] \tag{5.6}$$

$$= G[g_1(x_1) + \cdots + g_m(x_m)] \tag{5.7}$$

where

$$y_s = H_s[h_{1s}(x_{1s}) + \cdots + h_{ms}(x_{ms})](s = 1, \cdots, n) \qquad (5.8)$$

and

$$x_r = G_r[g_{r1}(x_{r1}) + \cdots + g_{rn}(x_{rn})](r = 1, \cdots, m) \qquad (5.9)$$

Proof: The sufficiency of the existence of the functions described is obvious. The proof of necessity will be given in four parts.

(i) It follows from equations (5.5) that consistent aggregation requires, for all $q, r = 1, \cdots, m$ and $s, t = 1, \cdots, n$, that

$$\frac{\dfrac{\partial y}{\partial y_s}}{\dfrac{\partial y}{\partial y_t}} = \frac{\dfrac{\partial x_q}{\partial x_{qs}}}{\dfrac{\partial f_s}{\partial x_{qs}}} \div \frac{\dfrac{\partial x_q}{\partial x_{qt}}}{\dfrac{\partial f_t}{\partial x_{qt}}} = \frac{\dfrac{\partial x_r}{\partial x_{rs}}}{\dfrac{\partial f_s}{\partial x_{rs}}} \div \frac{\dfrac{\partial x_r}{\partial x_{rt}}}{\dfrac{\partial f_t}{\partial x_{rt}}}$$

Consider the second expression. Examination of the functions (5.1) and (5.4) will show that of the partial derivatives in this expression

$\dfrac{\partial x_q}{\partial x_{qs}}$ and $\dfrac{\partial x_q}{\partial x_{qt}}$ depend only on the values of $x_{q1}, \cdots, x_{qn}$;

$\dfrac{\partial f_s}{\partial x_{qs}}$ and $\dfrac{\partial f_t}{\partial x_{qt}}$ depend only on the values of $x_{1s}, \cdots, x_{ms}$ and $x_{1t}, \cdots, x_{mt}$.

In the third expression

$\dfrac{\partial x_r}{\partial x_{rs}}$ and $\dfrac{\partial x_r}{\partial x_{rt}}$ depend only on the values of $x_{r1}, \cdots, x_{rn}$;

$\dfrac{\partial f_s}{\partial x_{rs}}$ and $\dfrac{\partial f_t}{\partial x_{rt}}$ depend only on the values of $x_{1s}, \cdots, x_{ms}$ and $x_{1t}, \cdots, x_{mt}$.

Hence the only variables on which both expressions depend are $x_{1s}, \cdots, x_{ms}$ and $x_{1t}, \cdots, x_{mt}$. These variables determine the values of y_s and y_t, by equations (5.1), but do not influence the value of any other y_i ($i \neq s, t$). Hence $(\partial y/\partial y_s)/(\partial y/\partial y_t)$, which is equal in value to both expressions, is a function only of y_s and y_t.

This result holds for all s and t, so that we can apply Theorem 2 of Chapter 3 to the function $y(y_1, \cdots, y_n)$, and deduce the existence of functions $H, h_1, \cdots, h_n$ such that

$$y = y(y_1, \cdots, y_n) = H[h_1(y_1) + \cdots + h_n(y_n)].$$

(ii) From equations (5.5), for all q, r, s, t:

$$\frac{\dfrac{\partial F}{\partial x_q}}{\dfrac{\partial F}{\partial x_r}} = \frac{\dfrac{\partial f_s}{\partial x_{qs}}}{\dfrac{\partial x_q}{\partial x_{qs}}} \div \frac{\dfrac{\partial f_s}{\partial x_{rs}}}{\dfrac{\partial x_r}{\partial x_{rs}}} = \frac{\dfrac{\partial f_t}{\partial x_{qt}}}{\dfrac{\partial x_q}{\partial x_{qt}}} \div \frac{\dfrac{\partial f_t}{\partial x_{rt}}}{\dfrac{\partial x_r}{\partial x_{rt}}}$$

The partial derivatives in the second expression depend only on $x_{1s}, \cdots,$ $x_{ms}, x_{q1}, \cdots, x_{qn}$ and $x_{r1}, \cdots, x_{rn}$. Those in the third expression depend only on $x_{1t}, \cdots, x_{mt}, x_{q1}, \cdots, x_{qn}$ and $x_{r1}, \cdots, x_{rn}$. The only variables common to the two lists are: $x_{q1}, \cdots, x_{qn}$ which determine x_q, and $x_{r1}, \cdots, x_{rn}$ which determine x_r. Hence $(\partial F/\partial x_q)/(\partial F/\partial x_r)$ is unaffected by the value of any x_i other than x_q or x_r. This is true for all q and r, so that Theorem 2 implies the existence of functions $G, g_1, \cdots, g_m$ such that $y = F(x_1, \cdots, x_m) = G[g_1(x_1) + \cdots + g_m(x_m)]$.

(iii) Equations (5.5) give, for all q, r and s

$$\frac{\dfrac{\partial f_s}{\partial x_{qs}}}{\dfrac{\partial f_s}{\partial x_{rs}}} = \frac{\dfrac{\partial F}{\partial x_q}\dfrac{\partial x_q}{\partial x_{qs}}}{\dfrac{\partial F}{\partial x_r}\dfrac{\partial x_r}{\partial x_{rs}}}$$

The left-hand side depends only on $x_{1s}, \cdots, x_{ms}$. On the right-hand side, $(\partial F/\partial x_q)/(\partial F/\partial x_r)$ has been shown in part (ii) of the proof to depend only on $x_{q1}, \cdots, x_{qn}$ and $x_{r1}, \cdots, x_{rn}$; these are also the only variables on which $\partial x_q/\partial x_{qs}$ and $\partial x_r/\partial x_{rs}$ depend. The only variables on which both sides depend are therefore x_{qs} and x_{rs}. Hence the left-hand side is a function only of x_{qs} and x_{rs}. Since this is true for all q and r, we can apply Theorem 2 to obtain

$$y_s = f_s(x_{1s}, \cdots, x_{ms}) = H_s[h_{1s}(x_{1s}) + \cdots + h_{ms}(x_{ms})].$$

(iv) Equations (5.5) give, for all r, s and t

$$\frac{\dfrac{\partial x_r}{\partial x_{rs}}}{\dfrac{\partial x_r}{\partial x_{rt}}} = \frac{\dfrac{\partial y}{\partial y_s}\dfrac{\partial f_s}{\partial x_{rs}}}{\dfrac{\partial y}{\partial y_t}\dfrac{\partial f_t}{\partial x_{rt}}}$$

By an argument similar to that of part (iii) of the proof, making use of the results of part (i), it can be shown that the left-hand side of this equation depends only on x_{rs} and x_{rt}, so that by Theorem 2

$$x_r = x_r(x_{r1}, \cdots, x_{rn}) = G_r[g_{r1}(x_{r1}) + \cdots + g_{rn}(x_{rn})].$$

This completes the proof of Theorem 8.

4.

It should be pointed out that if the individual functions f_s are interpreted as production functions, they have somewhat restrictive properties.

In the first place, there is no mention of intermediate products. It is implicitly assumed that all outputs are final outputs and that all inputs are original or non-produced inputs. The problem of intermediate products in the aggregate production function will be discussed in Chapter 9.

Secondly, it appears that each firm produces a single product. Now of course the variables y_s may be thought of, if we choose, as *indices* of the firm's output of different goods. Provided that the value of such an index is related by a function of the form (5.1) to the firm's inputs, Theorem 8 may be applied as it stands.

Can any restrictions be placed on the form of such an index? Let us assume, as does Nataf, that each firm's production function can be expressed in the form

$$y_{s1} = \phi_s(y_{s2}, \cdots, y_{sn_s}, x_{1s}, \cdots, x_{ms})$$
(5.10)

where $y_{s1}, y_{s2}, \cdots, y_{sn_s}$ are the *outputs* that the firm can produce. We may then assume that $\partial \phi_s / \partial y_{si} < 0$ ($i = 2, \cdots, n_s$) and $\partial \phi_s / \partial x_{rs} > 0$ ($r = 1, \cdots, m$). If we now regard all the variables $y_{s2}, \cdots, y_{sn_s}$ as *inputs*, and require that it be possible to aggregate the functions (5.10), it follows from Theorem 8 that we must be able to write

$$y_{s1} = k_s[j_{s2}(y_{s2}) + \cdots + j_{sn_s}(y_{sn_s}) + h_{1s}(x_{1s}) + \cdots + h_{ms}(x_{ms})].$$

If, as seems reasonable, we assume that k_s', the derivative of k_s with respect to the sum $j_{s2}(y_{s2}) + \cdots + h_{ms}(x_{ms})$, is always positive, we may write

$$k_s^{-1}(y_{s1}) = j_{s2}(y_{s2}) + \cdots + h_{ms}(x_{ms})$$

or

$$k_s^{-1}(y_{s1}) - j_{s2}(y_{s2}) - \cdots j_{sn_s}(y_{sn_s}) = h_{1s}(x_{1s}) + \cdots + h_{ms}(x_{ms}).$$

This may be written as

$$y_s = J[i_{s1}(y_{s1}) + \cdots + i_{sn_s}(y_{sn_s})] = h_s[h_{1s}(x_{1s}) + \cdots + h_{ms}(x_{ms})].$$

The index of outputs of the sth firm, therefore, must also be expressible as a function of a sum of functions, one for each of the individual outputs.

5.

We now consider a number of applications of the results of the early parts of this chapter. We continue to assume that the variables x_{rs} are free to take on any non-negative values.

(a) Let us first suppose that all aggregates are assumed to be simple sums

$$y = \sum_{s=1}^{n} y_s; \qquad x_r = \sum_{s=1}^{n} x_{rs} \qquad (r = 1, \cdots, m).$$

Then for all r and s, $\partial y / \partial y_s = \partial x_r / \partial x_{rs} = 1$, so that by Theorem 7 the necessary conditions for consistent aggregation are that for all r, s and t

$$\frac{\partial F}{\partial x_r} = \frac{\partial f_s}{\partial x_{rs}} = \frac{\partial f_t}{\partial x_{rt}}.$$

Now $\partial F / \partial x_r$ depends only on the values of the totals $x_1, \cdots, x_m$; a given set of totals is consistent with an infinite number of allocations of those totals among individual households, firms, etc. The values of $\partial f_s / \partial x_{rs}$ must not only be equal for all s, but constant for all values of x_{rs}. Hence the individual functions must be linear with identical slopes

$$y_s = a_s + \sum_{r=1}^{m} b_r x_{rs}.$$

This condition is also sufficient, since

$$y = \sum_{s=1}^{n} y_s = \sum_{s=1}^{n} a_s + \sum_{s=1}^{n} \sum_{r=1}^{m} b_r x_{rs}$$

$$= \sum_{s=1}^{n} a_s + \sum_{r=1}^{m} b_r \left(\sum_{s=1}^{n} x_{rs} \right) = a + \sum_{r=1}^{m} b_r x_r.$$

This problem was discussed by Theil (1954, Ch. 2), with y_s interpreted as household consumption of sugar. Theil assumes the functions f_s to be linear, and shows that they must have identical slopes. Our result is a little more general in that we have shown that the functions f_s must be linear.

Our general result was obtained by Adelman and Lobo (1956), who interpreted the functions f_s as production functions (see also example (c) below, pp. 41–42).

(b) If we continue to require that $y = \sum_{s=1}^{n} y_s$, but permit the aggregates x_r to be weighted sums

$$x_r = \sum_{s=1}^{n} w_{rs} x_{rs}$$

we have, from Theorem 7

$$\frac{\partial F}{\partial x_r} = \frac{1}{w_{rs}} \frac{\partial f_s}{\partial x_{rs}} = \frac{1}{w_{rt}} \frac{\partial f_t}{x_{rt}}.$$

It is easily shown that the functions f_s must again be linear, but they need no longer have identical slopes. However, it is clearly necessary, if

$$y_s = a_s + \sum_{r=1}^{m} b_{rs} x_{rs} \quad \text{and} \quad y_t = a_t + \sum_{r=1}^{m} b_{rt} x_{rt},$$

that for all r, s and t

$$\frac{b_{rs}}{w_{rs}} = \frac{b_{rt}}{w_{rt}}.$$

In that case, we have

$$y = \sum_{s=1}^{n} y_s = \sum_{s=1}^{n} a_s + \sum_{r=1}^{m} \sum_{s=1}^{n} b_{rs} x_{rs}$$

$$= a + \sum_{r=1}^{m} \frac{b_{ri}}{w_{ri}} \left(\sum_{s=1}^{n} w_{rs} x_{rs} \right)$$

$$= a + \sum_{r=1}^{m} c_r x_r$$

where i can be any number from 1 to n.

This argument is in accord with Theil's theorem that a suitable selection of the weights w_{rs} makes consistent aggregation[3] possible for any set of linear functions f_s. If y_s is thought of as household consumption of sugar, and the variables x_{1s} represent incomes, then the weights w_{1s} are determined by the marginal propensities to consume sugar. Hence "aggregate income," $x_1 = \sum_{s=1}^{n} w_{1s} x_{1s}$ will in general be defined in a different way for each commodity considered; (see Theil (1954), p. 172). As Theil points out, however, (*op. cit.*, p. 181), if there are groups of households with (roughly) uniform marginal propensities to consume sugar, it will be very convenient to weight each *group's* total income by this marginal propensity, thus achieving (roughly) consistent aggregation.

(c) We might, on the other hand, require that $x_r = \sum_{s=1}^{n} x_{rs}$, but allow $y = \sum_{s=1}^{n} c_s y_s$. Then, by Theorem 7

$$\frac{\partial F}{\partial x_r} = c_s \frac{\partial f_s}{\partial x_{rs}} = c_t \frac{\partial f_t}{\partial x_{rt}}.$$

Again the functions f_s must be linear, and if

$$y_s = a_s + \sum_{r=1}^{m} b_{rs} x_{rs} \quad \text{and} \quad y_t = a_t + \sum_{r=1}^{m} b_{rt} x_{rt}$$

we must have, for all r, s and t

$$\frac{b_{rs}}{b_{rt}} = \frac{c_t}{c_s} \quad \text{or} \quad c_s b_{rs} = c_t b_{rt} = k_r.$$

In that case

$$y = \sum_{s=1}^{n} c_s y_s = \sum_{s=1}^{n} c_s a_s + \sum_{r=1}^{m} \sum_{s=1}^{n} c_s b_{rs} x_{rs}$$

$$= \sum_{s=1}^{n} c_s a_s + \sum_{r=1}^{m} k_r \left(\sum_{s=1}^{n} x_{rs} \right)$$

$$= a + \sum_{r=1}^{m} k_r x_r.$$

[3] Theil uses the term "perfect aggregation."

This analysis can be used to extend slightly the discussion of the Adelman-Lobo case mentioned at the end of the analysis of example (a), (p. 40 above). If the functions f_s are interpreted as production functions, it is reasonable to assume that with no inputs there is no output, so that $a_s = 0$ for all s. The requirements for consistent aggregation are then that all production functions are linear and homogeneous,[4] and that the isoquant surfaces are parallel hyperplanes, identical for all firms. The only difference between examples (a) and (c), as applied to this problem, is that in example (a) it is implied, and in example (c) it is not implied, that units of output y_s are defined in such a way that, if identical bundles of inputs are applied to two firms, equal numbers of units of output will be produced by the two firms.

This result on production functions depends crucially on the assumption that the variables x_{rs} are free to take arbitrary values. This assumption will be relaxed in the next chapter.

(d) In view of the demonstrated importance of linearity in the present context, what can be said about non-linear functions?

One very obvious case is that in which the logarithm of y_s is a linear function of the logarithms of the variables $x_{1s}, \ldots , x_{ms}$ ($y_s = a_s x_{1s}^{b_1} \cdots x_{ms}^{b_m}$; cf. Klein (1946a)). The argument relating to examples (a), (b) and (c) can be repeated word for word, with $\log y_s$ and $\log x_{rs}$ substituted for y_s and x_{rs}. The aggregates y and x_r are then products and weighted products; they are subject to the disadvantages that (a) although they may permit consistent aggregation, they are often of little intrinsic interest to the economist and (b) the value of such an aggregate is zero if any of its components is zero. It may be, however, that sums and products, arithmetic means and geometric means will move together; cf. Klein (1953, pp. 192, 221 ff., 265 ff., 270 ff.). This will be the case in particular if the variables in question obey the lognormal distribution (see Chapter 8 below).

(e) But suppose, for example, to take a set of functions more general than (5.1) above, that there is a set of prices $x_1, \cdots , x_m$, each of which affects the value of *each* of the variables y_s, and that the functions f_s are second-degree polynomials

$$y_s = a_s + \sum_{r=1}^{m} b_{rs} x_r + \sum_{q=1}^{m} \sum_{r=1}^{m} c_{qr \cdot s} x_q x_r \qquad (5.11)$$

and that we wish to write

$$y = \sum_{s=1}^{n} y_s, \qquad x = \sum_{r=1}^{m} x_r, \quad \text{and} \quad y = F(x).$$

---

[4] It is important to note that "linear and homogeneous" is *not* synonymous with "homogeneous of first degree." A function with the latter property need not be linear in its arguments.

We must have

$$dy = \sum_{s=1}^{n} dy_s = \sum_{r=1}^{m} \sum_{s=1}^{n} \frac{\partial f_s}{\partial x_r} dx_r$$

$$= \sum_{r=1}^{m} \frac{\partial F}{\partial x} dx_r$$

so that for all q, r and s

$$\frac{\partial F}{\partial x} = \frac{\partial f_s}{\partial x_q} = \frac{\partial f_s}{\partial x_r}.$$

Differentiation of equations (5.11) yields, for all q, r, s and t

$$b_{rs} + \sum_{q=1}^{m} c_{qr \cdot s} x_q = b_{qs} + \sum_{r=1}^{m} c_{rq \cdot s} x_r$$

$$= b_{rt} + \sum_{q=1}^{m} c_{qr \cdot t} x_q = b_{qt} + \sum_{r=1}^{m} c_{rq \cdot t} x_r.$$

Since the variables x_q and x_r can take on any values, we must have

For all q, r: $b_{qs} = b_{qt} = b_{rs} = b_{rt} = b$ for all s and t

For all o, p, q, r: $c_{op \cdot s} = c_{qr \cdot s} = c_{op \cdot t} = c_{qr \cdot t} = c$ for all s and t.

Then $y_s = a_s + bx + cx^2$, and $y = \sum_{s=1}^{n} a_s + nbx + ncx^2$.

(f) Theil has a proposal for circumventing the extreme stringency of the conditions discovered in the analysis of the polynomials of example (e). Let us return to the functions (5.1), $y_s = f_s(x_{1s}, \cdots, x_{ms})$, and assume that they are second-degree polynomials[5]

$$y_s = a_s + \sum_{r=1}^{m} b_{rs} x_{rs} + \sum_{q=1}^{m} \sum_{r=1}^{m} c_{qr \cdot s} x_{qs} x_{rs}.$$

Theil (1954, p. 150) would propose the use of weighted moments of first and second orders

$$M_r = \sum_{s=1}^{n} \beta_{rs} x_{rs}; \qquad M_{qr} = \sum_{s=1}^{n} \gamma_{qr \cdot s} x_{qs} x_{rs},$$

choosing the weights in such a way that

For each r, $b_{rs}/\beta_{rs} = b_r$ for each s
For all q and r, $c_{qr \cdot s}/\gamma_{qr \cdot s} = c_{qr}$ for each s.

It then follows that

$$y = \sum_{s=1}^{n} a_s + \sum_{r=1}^{m} b_r M_r + \sum_{q=1}^{m} \sum_{r=1}^{m} c_{qr} M_{qr}.$$

[5] Generalization to higher degrees is trivial, but tedious to write out.

III. AGGREGATION OF ECONOMIC RELATIONS

Aggregation is certainly consistent. The use of weighted moments is a natural extension of the use of weighted sums discussed in connection with example (b) above. In Chapter 8 below we shall consider cases in which a knowledge of the probability distributions of the variables involved may permit consistent aggregation to be achieved by the use of a limited number of unweighted moments.[6]

[6] In the case of example (f), of course, polynomials of higher degree would require a great proliferation of moments.

CHAPTER 6

Degrees of Freedom Restricted: Optimal Conditions of Exchange and Production

1.

We shall not dwell further on the conditions for consistent aggregation when the number of degrees of freedom is at a maximum. We offer Theorem 7 as a useful tool in the analysis of such problems.

We turn to the set of problems in which the functions (5.1) are interpreted as utility functions or production functions enjoying properties (a) and (b) of the functions (2.1) of Chapter 2. We saw in the last chapter that consistent aggregation of production functions in the case of maximum degrees of freedom requires (i) that all isoquant surfaces be parallel hyperplanes, identical for all firms, if aggregates are sums or weighted sums (examples (a) and (c)); (ii) that if the production functions are of the Cobb-Douglas variety, aggregates must be products or geometric means (example (d)).

In a controversy in *Econometrica*, Klein (1946a, 1946b) took the view that only technical relationships of the nature of our functions f, should be taken into account when aggregation is contemplated. May (1946, 1947) argued, on the other hand, that institutional as well as technical relationships should be admitted, and investigated the conditions for consistent aggregation on the assumption of perfect competition in all markets. He pointed out that the firm's production function itself is not a purely technical relationship, since it results from a decision-making process within the firm. Klein's comment, that May's procedure makes it impossible to trace the effects on the aggregates of a technological change in the production function of one firm or industry, will be considered in Chapter 9 below (pp. 70–71).

In this chapter we shall proceed in the spirit of May's position in the controversy. This implies a reduction in the number of degrees of freedom, and less stringent conditions for consistent aggregation.

2.

We assume that the optimal conditions for the distribution of given totals of commodities among individuals, or of factors among firms, are satisfied. The aggregates x_r are therefore defined as follows for $r = 1, \cdots, m$:

$$x_r = \sum_{s=1}^{n} x_{rs}.$$

It is well known that the necessary conditions for a maximum of y_s, given the values of all the other y_t's and of all the x_r's, are that, for all q, r, s and t

$$\frac{\dfrac{\partial f_s}{\partial x_{qs}}}{\dfrac{\partial f_s}{\partial x_{rs}}} = \frac{\dfrac{\partial f_t}{\partial x_{qt}}}{\dfrac{\partial f_t}{\partial x_{rt}}} \qquad (6.1)$$

The marginal rate of substitution between any two commodities (inputs) must be the same for any two individuals (firms).

There are mn variables x_{rs} and m aggregates x_r. There are $(m - 1)$ $(n - 1)$ optimal conditions (6.1) and m equations defining the aggregates x_r. This leaves $(m + n - 1)$ degrees of freedom. It follows that the implicit function

$$F(y_1, \cdots, y_n, x_1, \cdots, x_m) = 0 \qquad (6.2)$$

has the property that the value of any one of its $(m + n)$ arguments is uniquely determined by the values of all the others.

The function (6.2) may be used in a number of ways. If the y_s's are interpreted as utilities, then if we hold all the x_r's constant, the function

$$H_{\dot{x}}(y_1, \cdots, y_n) = 0 \qquad (6.3)$$

defines a utility-possibility surface (cf. Samuelson (1950)). If we hold all the y_s's constant, the function

$$G_{\dot{y}}(x_1, \cdots, x_m) = 0 \qquad (6.4)$$

defines a social indifference surface in the sense of Scitovsky (1942).

If the y's are interpreted as outputs, the function (6.3) defines a production possibility surface, and the function (6.4) defines a "required-inputs isoquant", as used by Dorfman, Samuelson, and Solow (1958, pp. 311–2) in their discussion of the turnpike theorem.

3.

In order to derive the conditions for consistent aggregation when the optimal conditions are satisfied, we recall that an essential step in the proof of Theorem 7 was the demonstration that the following condition is necessary:

$$\sum_{s=1}^{n} \sum_{r=1}^{m} \left(\frac{\partial F}{\partial x_r} \frac{\partial x_r}{\partial x_{rs}} - \frac{\partial y}{\partial y_s} \frac{\partial f_s}{\partial x_{rs}} \right) dx_{rs} = 0;$$

since $x_r = \sum_{s=1}^{n} x_{rs}$, this becomes

$$\sum_{s=1}^{n} \sum_{r=1}^{m} \left(\frac{\partial F}{\partial x_r} - \frac{\partial y}{\partial y_s} \frac{\partial f_s}{\partial x_{rs}} \right) dx_{rs} = 0.$$

The conditions (5.5) of Theorem 7 were established on the assumption that the variables x_{rs} were free to take any values. Now although it is true that the optimal conditions (6.1) restrict the allocation of *given* totals $x_1, \cdots, x_m$ among firms or individuals, the aggregation conditions must hold for all possible variations of the totals $x_1, \cdots, x_m$, and therefore for all variations in the values of the variables x_{rs}. It remains necessary for consistent aggregation, therefore, that for all r and s

$$\frac{\partial F}{\partial x_r} = \frac{\partial y}{\partial y_s} \frac{\partial f_s}{\partial x_{rs}}. \tag{6.5}$$

The conditions (6.5) are identical with those which would be required in the case of maximum degrees of freedom, with x_r defined as $\sum_{s=1}^{n} x_{rs}$. We assume in this chapter, however, that the optimal conditions (6.1) are satisfied, and that indifference surfaces and iso-product surfaces are smoothly convex to the origin. We shall find that in these conditions it is necessary (Theorem 9) and sufficient (Theorem 10), for consistent aggregation of the functions f_s to the function $y = F(x_1, \cdots, x_m)$, that all Engel curves or expansion paths are straight lines, parallel for all individuals or firms. These theorems are the work of Gorman (1953).

We shall also find, in contrast to examples (a) and (c) of Chapter 5, that in the case of the aggregate production function with y defined as $\sum_{s=1}^{n} y_s$ or $\sum_{s=1}^{n} c_s y_s$, the assumptions of this chapter make the linearity of the individual production functions unnecessary.

4.

THEOREM 9: *It is necessary for consistent aggregation, when the optimal conditions (6.1) are satisfied, that: (a) for each firm or individual, each set of points, in output or commodity space, at which marginal rates of substitution are constant,[1] is a straight line; (b) for a given set of marginal rates of substitution, the straight lines for all individuals or firms are parallel.*

Proof: Let us write X_s for the vector of individual quantities $(x_{1s}, \cdots, x_{ms})$ and X for the vector of totals $(x_1, \cdots, x_m)$. It is a consequence of the "Hicksian stability conditions" on the functions f_s, that the marginal rate of substitution between any two individual variables x_{qs} and x_{rs} is uniquely determined by the vector of values $X_s = (x_{1s}, \cdots, x_{ms})$. If we write R_s for the vectors of marginal rates of substitution

$$R_s = \left[\frac{\dfrac{\partial f_s}{\partial x_{2s}}}{\dfrac{\partial f_s}{\partial x_{1s}}}, \cdots, \frac{\dfrac{\partial f_s}{\partial x_{ms}}}{\dfrac{\partial f_s}{\partial x_{1s}}} \right]$$

we can write down the vector equation $R_s = R_s(X_s)$.[2]

---

[1] That is, each Engel curve or expansion path.

[2] This means that to each vector X_s there corresponds a unique vector R_s.

We can also write

$$R_1(X_1) = R_2(X_2) = \cdots = R_n(X_n) = R(X). \qquad (6.6)$$

The first $(n - 1)$ equalities of (6.6) are a direct consequence of the optimal conditions (6.1). The last equality says that the common vector of marginal rates of substitution R, is uniquely determined by the totals $x_1, \cdots, x_m$. This is true because (6.5) implies, for all q, r, s and t:

$$\frac{\dfrac{\partial F}{\partial x_q}}{\dfrac{\partial F}{\partial x_r}} = \frac{\dfrac{\partial f_s}{\partial x_{qs}}}{\dfrac{\partial f_s}{\partial x_{rs}}} = \frac{\dfrac{\partial f_t}{\partial x_{qt}}}{\dfrac{\partial f_t}{\partial x_{rt}}}$$

Since the first expression depends only on the totals $x_1, \cdots, x_m$, the same must be true of the common marginal rate of substitution.

Let us now change one of the individual vectors, X_s to $X_s + dX = (x_{1s} + dx_1, \cdots, x_{ms} + dx_m)$, leaving the other $(n - 1)$ individual vectors unchanged, but of course changing the vector of totals to $X + dX$. Let us suppose that the vector of marginal rates of substitution R_s is unaffected by this change, so that

$$R_1(X_1) = \cdots = R_s(X_s + dX) = \cdots = R_n(X_n) = R(X + dX) = R(X).$$

Let us now transfer dX from s to t. We shall show that $R_t(X_t + dX) = R_t(X_t)$.

If it were not so, we should have

$$R_1(X_1) = \cdots = R_s(X_s) = \cdots = R_n(X_n) = R(X + dX) \neq R_t(X_t + dX).$$

This distribution of $X + dX$ is clearly not optimal. It must be possible to improve on it by holding constant all values of y_s but one and maximizing the remaining one. But this procedure must change (for example) the vector X_s while holding y_s constant; such a movement along an indifference surface or an iso-product surface must, by the Hicksian stability conditions, change the vector of marginal rates of substitution R_s. Hence the new optimum allocation of the given vector of totals $(X + dX)$ will involve a different common vector of marginal rates of substitution. This contradiction establishes that $R_t(X_t) = R_t(X_t + dX)$.

By returning to the vectors X_s and X_t, we can show by a similar argument that $R_s(X_s - dX) = R_t(X_t + dX)$.

We have shown that, for all s and t:

If $R_s(X_s) = R_s(X_s + dX) = R_t(X_t)$, then $R_t(X_t + dX) = R_t(X_t)$ (that is, the Engel curves and expansion paths of s and t are parallel).

If $R_s(X_s) = R_s(X_s + dX)$, then $R_s(X_s) = R_s(X_s - dX)$ (that is, the Engel curves and expansion paths are straight lines).

5.

It is clear that if the utility and production functions f_s are defined for all non-negative values of $x_{1s}, \cdots, x_{ms}$, and if the optimal conditions (6.1) hold for all possible values of the totals $x_1, \cdots, x_m$, then the Engel curves and expansion paths must not only be straight and parallel, but must also pass through their respective origins. We shall assume this to be the case in Theorem 10; an interesting case considered by Gorman (1953), where it is assumed that each individual has a certain minimum level of consumption, below which his utility function is not defined, will be considered at the end of this chapter.

THEOREM 10: *If the Engel curves or expansion paths for all individuals or firms, at a given set of commodity or input prices, are parallel straight lines through their origins, then consistent aggregation of the functions $f_s(x_{1s}, \cdots, x_{ms})$ to the function $y = F(x_1, \cdots, x_m)$ is possible.*

Moreover, there exist functions F and $h_1, \cdots, h_m$ such that

$$y = \sum_{s=1}^{n} h_s(y_s) = F(x_1, \cdots, x_m)$$

where the function F is homogeneous of degree one in its arguments.

Proof: The Hicksian stability conditions imply that for any level of utility or output y_s, and for any vector of marginal rates of substitution R_s, the value of each x_{rs} is uniquely determined. But if Engel curves or expansion paths are straight lines through the origin, the marginal rates of substitution depend only on the ratios $x_{1s}/x_{rs}, \cdots, x_{ms}/x_{rs}$. And if all Engel curves and expansion paths are parallel, the optimal ratios will be the same for all s, and equal to the ratios of the totals $x_1/x_r, \cdots, x_m/x_r$.

Hence for each r and s, x_{rs} depends only on y_s and the ratios $x_1/x_r, \cdots, x_m/x_r$;

$$x_{rs} = k_{rs}\left(y_s, \frac{x_1}{x_r}, \cdots, \frac{x_m}{x_r}\right).$$

Given any particular set of ratios, $(x_1/x_r)_0, \cdots, (x_m/x_r)_0$, x_{rs} is a function of y_s alone

$$x_{rs} = k_{rs}^0(y_s): \qquad x_r = \sum_{s=1}^{n} x_{rs} = \sum_{s=1}^{n} k_{rs}^0(y_s).$$

Now the indifference surfaces and iso-product surfaces are, by hypothesis, identical for all individuals or firms, and homothetic[3] with

---

[3] If two figures A and B are "homothetic," or "similarly placed," with reference to a point P, then for any two straight lines PQR and $PQ'R'$ through P, cutting A in Q and Q' and B in R and R', the ratios PQ/PR and PQ'/PR' are equal. The most familiar example of homothetic surfaces in economics is the set of isoquants associated with a constant-returns-to-scale production function.

respect to their origins. Thus a change in the ratios $x_1/x_r, \cdots, x_m/x_r$, and the associated change in the common marginal rates of substitution, will change, in the same proportion for each s, the value of x_{rs} associated with a given utility or output y_s. This proportion will be a function of the ratios $x_1/x_r, \cdots, x_m/x_r$. Hence

$$x_r = \sum_{s=1}^{n} k_{rs}^0(y_s) \cdot G\left(\frac{x_1}{x_r}, \cdots, \frac{x_m}{x_r}\right),$$

$$y = \sum_{s=1}^{n} k_{rs}^0(y_s) = \frac{x_r}{G\left(\dfrac{x_1}{x_r}, \cdots, \dfrac{x_m}{x_r}\right)}.$$

The last expression is clearly homogeneous of degree one in $x_1, \cdots, x_m$.

6.

Let us now reconsider the case of the aggregate production function (cf. examples (a) and (c) of Chapter 5), where we wish to define y as $\sum_{s=1}^{n} y_s$ or as $\sum_{s=1}^{n} c_s y_s$. The following Corollary to Theorem 10 shows that, if the optimal conditions (6.1) are satisfied, it is sufficient that the individual production functions are homogeneous of degree one; they must still, of course, have parallel expansion paths at a given set of factor prices.

COROLLARY TO THEOREM 10: *If the conditions of Theorem 10 are satisfied, and each of the functions f_s is homogeneous of degree one, consistent aggregation is possible with $y = \sum_{s=1}^{n} c_s y_s$.*

Proof: In this case, each x_{rs}, given the marginal rates of substitution, is proportional to y_s, so that

$$x_r = \sum_{s=1}^{n} x_{rs} = \sum_{s=1}^{n} c_{rs}^0 \cdot y_s \cdot G\left(\frac{x_1}{x_r}, \cdots, \frac{x_m}{x_r}\right);$$

$$y = \sum_{s=1}^{n} c_{rs}^0 \cdot y_s = \frac{x_r}{G\left(\dfrac{x_1}{x_r}, \cdots, \dfrac{x_m}{x_r}\right)}.$$

Let us again take the Cobb-Douglas function as an example

$$y_s = A_s x_{1s}^{b_{1s}} \cdots x_{ms}^{b_{ms}}$$

where $\sum_{r=1}^{m} b_{rs} = 1$. The conditions of Theorem 10 mean that for each r, $b_{rs} = b_{rt} = b_r$ for all s and t. In this case, the optimal input proportions are the same for all firms. Hence:

$$y_s = A_s x_{1s} \left(\frac{x_{2s}}{x_{1s}}\right)^{b_2} \cdots \left(\frac{x_{ms}}{x_{1s}}\right)^{b_m} = A_s x_{1s} \left(\frac{x_2}{x_1}\right)^{b_2} \cdots \left(\frac{x_m}{x_1}\right)^{b_m}$$

$$y = \sum_{s=1}^{n} \frac{y_s}{A_s} = \sum_{s=1}^{n} x_{1s} \left(\frac{x_2}{x_1}\right)^{b_2} \cdots \left(\frac{x_m}{x_1}\right)^{b_m} = x_1 \left(\frac{x_2}{x_1}\right)^{b_2} \cdots \left(\frac{x_m}{x_1}\right)^{b_m}$$

$$= x_1^{b_1} x_2^{b_2} \cdots x_m^{b_m}.$$

The production-possibility surfaces are of course hyperplanes, and the coefficients A_s are inversely proportional to the marginal costs of the outputs.

7.

Let us now consider Gorman's case of utility functions undefined for some batches of goods. It is assumed that for each individual there is a minimal level of consumption, which may be assumed to be attained by consuming various combinations of commodities lying on an indifference surface which is smoothly convex to the origin.

If we follow the steps in the proof of Theorem 10, we note first that, for a given level of utility y_s, the consumption x_{rs} of the rth commodity depends on the vector of marginal rates of substitution, common to all individuals and uniquely determined by the totals $x_1, \cdots, x_m$. We can *not*, in this case, show that they depend only on the *ratios* of the totals. Hence

$$x_{rs} = k_{rs}(y_s, x_1, \cdots, x_m).$$

For a given set of totals, $x_1^0, \cdots, x_m^0$, x_{rs} is a function of y_s alone:

$$x_{rs} = k_{rs}^0(y_s).$$

The Engel curves, which must be straight lines parallel for all individuals, lead upward not from the origins but from the minimal indifference surfaces. When the totals $x_1, \cdots, x_m$ change, and with them the common marginal rates of substitution, the quantities which, given y_s, are changed in the same proportion for all s are now not the quantities x_{rs} themselves, but the *excess* of x_{rs} over the amounts consumed on the minimal indifference surfaces. Thus if we write y_s^M as the level of utility reached on the minimal indifference surface, and $G(x_1, \cdots, x_m)$ for the common proportion in which the excess is changed, we have

$$x_{rs} - k_{rs}(y_s^M, x_1, \cdots, x_m) = [k_{rs}^0(y_s) - k_{rs}^0(y_s^M)] \cdot G(x_1, \cdots, x_m)$$

and

$$y = \sum_{s=1}^{n} [k_{rs}^0(y_s) - k_{rs}^0(y_s^M)] = \frac{x_r - \sum_{s=1}^{n} k_{rs}(y_s^M, x_1, \cdots, x_m)}{G(x_1, \cdots, x_m)}.$$

If we define individual utility as $k_{rs}^0(y_s) - k_{rs}^0(y_s^M)$, we see that "social utility" can, as in Theorem 10, be written as a sum of functions of individual utilities. But the final expression shows that in this case the aggregate function $F(x_1, \cdots, x_m)$ is *not* in general homogeneous of degree one.

CHAPTER 7

Aggregation when Optimal Conditions of Production or Exchange are Satisfied: Discussion

1.

After the somewhat technical arguments of the preceding chapter, we pause to consider the economic significance of its main results. We sought the conditions in which consistent aggregation of the individual utility or production functions $f_s(x_{1s}, \cdots, x_{ms})$ to the function $F(x_1, \cdots, x_m)$ is possible, if x_r is defined as $\sum_{s=1}^{n} x_{rs}$, and the optimal conditions of exchange or production are satisfied. One way of expressing the results of Theorems 9 and 10 of Chapter 6 is that it is necessary and sufficient for consistent aggregation[1] that there should exist some function, say f, which is homogeneous of degree one in the m commodities or inputs, and that each of the individual utility or production functions should be expressible as a function of f. In the Cobb-Douglas example considered on page 42 above, where we assumed that $y_s = A_s x_{1s}^{b_1} \cdots x_{ms}^{b_m}$, the common function f was the function $x_{1s}^{b_1} \cdots x_{ms}^{b_m}$, and each of the functions f_s was a constant multiple of f.

Let us write, in general

$$y_s = f_s(x_{1s}, \cdots, x_{ms}) = g_s[f(x_{1s}, \cdots, x_{ms})]$$

where f is the "common" function, homogeneous of degree one. Since it has been assumed that, for all r and s, $\partial f_s/\partial x_{rs} > 0$, we assume also that $\partial f/\partial x_{rs} > 0$, which implies that $dg_s/df > 0$. The indifference surfaces or iso-product surfaces of the functions f_s, everywhere smoothly convex to the origin by virtue of the Hicksian stability conditions, are identical with those of the common function f and of the aggregate function F.

2.

Let us first consider the relationship of the results obtained in Chapter 6 with the analysis of grouping of variables in Chapter 2–4.

Suppose that the common function f admits the following grouping of variables:

$$f(x_{1s}, \cdots, x_{ms}) = \phi[X_1(x_{1s}, \cdots, x_{gs}), X_2(x_{hs}, \cdots, x_{ms})].$$

Then clearly

$$f_s = g_s(f) = g_s\{\phi[X_1(x_{1s}, \cdots, x_{gs}), X_2(x_{hs}, \cdots, x_{ms})]\}.$$

---

[1] The result stated here holds if all the individual functions are assumed to be defined, and the optimal conditions are assumed to hold, for all non-negative values of the relevant variables.

On the other hand, if

$$f_s(x_{1s}, \cdots , x_{ms}) = \phi_s[X_1(x_{1s}, \cdots , x_{gs}), X_2(x_{hs}, \cdots , x_{ms})]$$

then

$$f(x_{1s}, \cdots , x_{ms}) = g_s^{-1}\{\phi_s[X_1(x_{1s}, \cdots , x_{gs}), X_2(x_{hs}, \cdots , x_{ms})]\}^{\dagger}$$

Grouping of variables by means of the functions X_1 and X_2 in the individual functions f_s is possible if and only if the variables can be grouped by the same functions X_1 and X_2 in the common function f.

We found in Chapter 4 that the condition for the quantity-indices to be treated in all respects like elementary variables was that all the grouping functions (here X_1 and X_2) should be homogeneous of degree one in their arguments. If this is the case we have (bearing in mind that the common function f is homogeneous of degree one)

$$\lambda f = f(\lambda x_{1s}, \cdots , \lambda x_{gs}, \lambda x_{hs}, \cdots , \lambda x_{ms})$$
$$= \phi[X_1(\lambda x_{1s}, \cdots , \lambda x_{gs}), X_2(\lambda x_{hs}, \cdots , \lambda x_{ms})]$$
$$= \phi[\lambda X_1, \lambda X_2].$$

Hence if the grouping functions X_1 and X_2 are homogeneous of degree one, the common function f is homogeneous of degree one in the grouped variables X_1 and X_2.

We have shown that if aggregation of the ungrouped functions f_s is consistent, and grouping of variables in the full sense of Chapter 4 is possible, the way in which variables are grouped must be the same for all the individual functions f_s. Aggregation of the grouped functions ϕ_s will then also be consistent.

3.

Let us now ask whether the aggregation of utility or production functions discussed in Chapter 6 is useful, on the unlikely assumption that the conditions for consistent aggregation are satisfied. We recall that in Chapter 4 several of our examples were taken to relate to household demand for sugar. The results were assumed to be of interest because total demand (the sum of individual demands) for sugar may be of interest to the economist—it may be an "intrinsic" aggregate in Malinvaud's sense (1956a).

Can the same be said of the aggregates y which can be constructed if the conditions of Theorems 9 and 10 are satisfied? What intrinsic interest attaches to an aggregate of utility or output which can be written as a sum of functions of individual utilities or outputs?

---

† Since it has been assumed that $dg_s/df > 0$ everywhere, we are entitled to write f as a function of f_s: $f = g_s^{-1}(f_s)$. Generalization of the argument to the case of more than two groups is of course trivial.

In the case of utility, we cannot of course say unambiguously that social welfare has increased if y expressed as a function of $x_1, \cdots, x_m$ has risen. Such a statement could be made only on the basis of a Bergson social welfare function (cf. Samuelson (1947, Ch. VIII)), with individual utilities as its arguments:

$$W = W(y_1, \cdots, y_n).$$

If we maximize this, given the possibilities defined by the transformation function (6.2) with $(m + n - 1)$ degrees of freedom, $F(y_1, \cdots, y_n, x_1, \cdots, x_m) = 0$, we obtain the $(n - 1)$ conditions

$$\frac{\partial W}{\partial y_s} \Big/ \frac{\partial W}{\partial y_t} = \frac{\partial F}{\partial y_s} \Big/ \frac{\partial F}{\partial y_t}.$$

The number of degrees of freedom is thus reduced to m, and we may write social utility directly as a function of commodity totals

$$W = U(x_1, \cdots, x_m) \tag{7.1}$$

without reference to the aggregation conditions of Chapter 6.

Moreover, the function (7.1) thus obtained, regarded now as a function of *outputs*, can be maximized subject to the transformation function (6.2), regarded as a relationship between outputs and total inputs. This will yield a function expressing social utility as a function of input totals. (See Chapter 13 below).

4.

The assumption that a known Bergson social welfare function is maximized would render the aggregation conditions of Chapter 6 superfluous. But if we do not know the Bergson social welfare function, the conditions derived in Chapter 6, as they relate to utility functions, ensure that utility possibility curves, showing the combinations of individual utilities derivable from a given set of commodity totals, will never intersect each other.

If the conditions of Chapter 6 are satisfied by production functions, they ensure that no two production possibility surfaces will ever intersect. This implies in turn that no two utility possibility surfaces, defined now as showing the combinations of utilities derivable from the outputs of a given set of *input* totals, will never intersect; this will be true whether or not the conditions for consistent aggregation are satisfied by the utility functions.

In either case an increase in y, whether as a function of commodity totals or of input totals, will indicate a "potential improvement" in the sense of Samuelson (1950). Figure 1 illustrates this for the case of two consumers, with utilities y_1 and y_2. The change from $U_1 U_1'$ to $U_2 U_2'$

constitutes a "potential improvement" in that the utility possibility curve for situation 2 (whether it be derived from given commodity totals or from given input totals) lies uniformly outside that for situation 1.

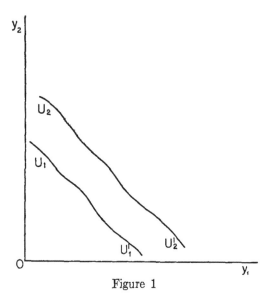

Figure 1

The significance of such statements as "aggregate output has increased by 5%" will be considered in a further discussion of the aggregate production function in Chapter 13 below.

5.

There is, however, a further important implication of the aggregation conditions of Chapter 6—namely that if they are satisfied, the determination of the values of certain aggregates can be interpreted in terms of a theory analogous to the theory of individual behaviour.

If we interpret the individual functions f_s as utility functions, the conditions of Theorem 9 and 10 imply that the total demand for each commodity is determined by prices and total income. This is easily seen, since if Engel curves are straight and parallel, a redistribution of money income with given commodity prices will increase some demands and decrease others, but leave total demand unchanged. The aggregation conditions of Chapter 6 are, in fact, the necessary and sufficient conditions for consistent aggregation in example (a) of Chapter 5 (p. 39 above). Samuelson (1956) suggests that one of the main reasons for concern with social indifference curves is precisely its bearing on the problem of market demand curves.

In the same vein, interpreting the functions f_s as production functions, consider the Corollary to Theorem 10. If each individual production function is homogeneous of degree one, then in conditions of perfect competition the wage of the rth factor in the sth firm will be

$$w_r = p_s \frac{\partial f_s}{\partial x_{rs}} \tag{7.2}$$

where p_s is the price of y_s. If each factor is paid such a wage, the value of the output of the sth firm, $p_s y_s$, will be exactly distributed. The Corollary shows that in this case y may be written as $\sum_{s=1}^{n} c_s y_s$, and it is plain that in perfect competition the constants c_s will be proportional to the prices p_s. Let us therefore write $p_s = p \cdot c_s$, where p is the price of output in general. Then we have, making use of (7.2) and (6.5)

$$\frac{\partial F}{\partial x_r} = \frac{\partial y}{\partial y_s} \frac{\partial f_s}{\partial x_{rs}} = c_s \frac{w_r}{p_s} = \frac{w_r}{p}$$

so that $w_r = p(\partial F / \partial x_r)$. The wage of the rth factor can be derived from the aggregate production function, which was shown in Theorem 10 to be homogeneous of first degree. The wage w_r thus obtained is the same as that paid by the individual firms, and the payment of such wages exactly exhausts individual outputs and, therefore, the value of aggregate output $p \cdot y = \sum_{s=1}^{n} p_s y_s$.

6.

There is a considerable body of literature on that aspect of the aggregation problem which relates to price-indices. In his survey article, Frisch (1936) distinguishes two approaches to the problem. The "atomistic" approach, concerned with the satisfaction of "chain" tests, "base-reversal" tests and the like, is familiar from the work of Fisher (1922) and the statistics textbooks. Such analyses are not firmly based on economic theory; the same may be said of the celebrated Divisia indices (1925-6). The "functional" approach, of which Frisch was himself a pioneer (and which is ably surveyed by Ulmer (1949)), is more in keeping with the analysis of the present volume. A good statement of the requirements for a functional price-index is that of Nataf and Roy (1948, p. 331)

The price-index z, for a given consumer and a given set of prices, is such that the standard of living of the consumer will not be changed if, his income remaining the same, the base prices are all multiplied by z.[2]

[2] My translation.

This implies that the utility enjoyed by a consumer must be expressible as a function of income and the price-index alone. It must be possible to write the "indirect" utility function of Chapter 3

$$U = \phi(E, p_1, \cdots, p_m)$$

in the form

$$U = G[E, P(p_1, \cdots, p_m)].$$

By virtue of an argument used in the proof of Theorem 3, (p. 23 above) it is necessary that, for all q and r

$$\frac{\dfrac{\partial G}{\partial p_q}}{\dfrac{\partial G}{\partial p_r}} = G_{qr}(p_1, \cdots, p_m) = \frac{x_q}{x_r}$$

so that Engel curves are straight lines through the origin. The direct utility function, expressed in terms of the quantities $x_1, \cdots, x_m$, is therefore homogeneous of degree one. We found in Theorem 4 that in this case we could write

$$u = \frac{E}{P(p_1, \cdots, p_m)} \tag{7.3}$$

with P, the price index, homogeneous of degree one.

The condition (7.3) is just what Nataf and Roy require. If the conditions of Theorem 10 hold, so that Engel curves are straight and parallel for all individuals, we may consider (7.3) as applying to individuals, so that

$$u_s = \frac{E_s}{P(p_1, \cdots, p_m)}.$$

If we now define "social utility," in direct form, as $\sum_{s=1}^{n} u_s$, we have

$$u = \sum_{s=1}^{n} u_s = \frac{E}{P(p_1, \cdots, p_m)}$$

and division of total income by the price index will indicate whether "social utility" is rising or falling (though of course only in the sense of "potential improvement" discussed earlier in this chapter). The analysis of the Cobb-Douglas utility function on p. 27 above will serve as an illustration here.

7.

We conclude with a brief note on the relationship of the results of Chapter 6 to the work of Arrow (1951). His investigation of the possibility of deriving a social preference scale from individual preference scales is certainly related to the problem of aggregation in the broadest sense (cf. the first sentence of Chapter 1 above). Our investigation is limited to the case where such preference scales are representable by differentiable functions.

We have found, however, that aggregation of utility functions requires indifference surfaces which are homothetic to the origin and identical for all individuals. We have said that a combination of commodity totals $x_1, \cdots, x_m$ lying on a higher indifference surface represents a higher social utility (in the limited sense of Samuelson's "potential improvement"). Any two points on the same social indifference surface may be regarded, as far as our aggregate measure is concerned, as socially equivalent.

Such a situation would appear to correspond to what Arrow describes as the "one-commodity world" (*op. cit.*, p. 69):

> "We then order any two social states with different total outputs in accordance with the total output, any two states with the same output according to the arbitrary ordering. This sets up a genuine weak ordering which does not coincide with the ordering of any one individual."

Though our social utility function meets Arrow's requirements, the conditions in which it exists constitute a degenerate case of his problem.

8.

So much for the aggregation conditions when the degrees of freedom are limited only by the optimal conditions of production or exchange. The conditions for consistent aggregation are only a little less stringent than when the degrees of freedom are at a maximum. In the next chapter we consider further sources of reduction in the number of degrees of freedom, with a consequent lightening of the conditions for consistent aggregation.

CHAPTER 8

Other Restrictions on the Number of Degrees of Freedom

1.

It would be very convenient if the "independent" variables x_{rs} of the equations (5.1) obeyed mn relations of the following type:

$$x_{rs} = f_{rs}(x_r)$$

for then we could write

$$y = y(y_1, \cdots, y_n) = y[f_1(x_{11}, \cdots, x_{m1}), \cdots, f_n(x_{1n}, \cdots, x_{mn})]$$

$$= y\{f_1[f_{11}(x_1), \cdots, f_{m1}(x_m)], \cdots, f_n[f_{1n}(x_1), \cdots, f_{mn}(x_m)]\}$$

$$= F(x_1, \cdots, x_m).$$

Consistent aggregation is then possible irrespective of the form of the function $y(y_1, \cdots, y_n)$, but the forms of the functions $f_{rs}(x_r)$ and $x_r(x_{r1}, \cdots, x_{rn})$ are not independent. For example, if we define x_r as $\sum_{s=1}^{n} x_{rs}$, the functions f_{rs} must be of the form

$$x_{rs} = g_{rs}(x_r) + b_{rs} \cdot x_r$$

where $\sum_{s=1}^{n} g_{rs}(x_r) = 0$ and $\sum_{s=1}^{n} b_{rs} = 1$.

An instance is provided by the household sugar consumption example of Chapter 5 (example (a), p. 40). If all incomes move proportionally, then $x_{rs} = b_{rs}x_r$, and total consumption is a function of total income. The assumption that incomes do move roughly in proportion underlies Stone's use of aggregate demand functions (1954, p. 253).

2.

But a word of caution must be issued. Even if a given proportional distribution of money income is maintained, it does *not* necessarily permit the aggregation of individual utility functions to a social utility function. Unless the individual utility functions have special properties, the social indifference surfaces derived on the assumption of a fixed proportional distribution of money income may intersect.

It is for this reason that Samuelson (1956) describes the rule that money incomes should be distributed in a fixed pattern as a "shibboleth"—such a rule does not lead to a consistent social ordering of commodity bundles. Moreover, since social indifference surfaces may intersect, the "substitution theorem" of consumption theory (that a compensated increase in the price of a commodity will not increase the

61

quantity demanded) may fail to be satisfied by aggregate demand functions even though it is satisfied by each individual demand function. This may be shown by a geometric illustration (Fig. 2).

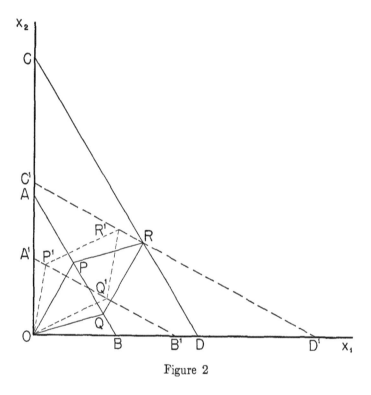

Figure 2

The incomes of two individuals are assumed to be equal, and the prices of commodities x_1 and x_2 are represented initially by the slope of the common individual budget line AB. Individual demands are represented by the points P and Q, and the resultant total demand is represented on the "community" budget line CD by the point R. Now let the individual and community budget lines shift to $A'B'$ and $C'D'$ respectively. The shifts in individual demands to P' and Q' are consistent, in that neither involves the choice of a combination of x_1 and x_2 that has previously been rejected. The change in total demand from R to R', however, is inconsistent, since the "community" now chooses the point R', which it had previously rejected in favour of R. (Note that it is not necessary to assume, in order to obtain this result, that either x_1 or x_2 is an inferior good for either individual.)

It may be verified by adding the appropriate lines to Fig. 2 that if both Engel curves are straight lines through the origin, then this inconsistency cannot occur. This was proved for the general case by Nataf and Roy (1948, pp. 342–3), and a version of the proof follows.

We have shown earlier (Theorem 4; see also pp. 57–58 above) that the assumption of straight Engel curves through the origin implies that individual utility can be written in indirect form as

$$u_s = \frac{E_s}{P_s(p_1, \cdots, p_m)}$$

where E_s is expenditure by individual s, and P_s is the price-index (homogeneous of first degree) appropriate to him. If we define v_s as $\log u_s$, and assume that incomes move proportionally, so that $E_s = a_s \cdot E$, we have

$$v_s = \log E_s - \log P_s = \log a_s + \log E - \log P_s$$

$$= \log E + \log \frac{a_s}{P_s}.$$

If we now define v as $1/n \sum_{s=1}^{n} v_s$

$$v = \frac{1}{n}(n \log E) + \frac{1}{n} \sum_{s=1}^{n} \log \frac{a_s}{P_s}$$

$$= \log E - \log P(p_1, \cdots, p_m)$$

where P is homogeneous of degree one in $p_1, \cdots, p_m$, since it is the nth root of the product of n functions P_s/a_s, each of which is homogeneous of degree one in $p_1, \cdots, p_m$. Defining u as antilog v, we can write

$$u = \frac{E}{P(p_1, \cdots, p_m)}$$

which defines a social utility function with non-intersecting indifference surfaces homothetic with reference to the origin.

The general necessary conditions for the existence of a social utility function when incomes are all equal have been presented by Nataf (1953, pp. 31 ff.) in a regrettably little-known paper.

3.

Let us now return to the case where no optimal conditions are imposed on the variables x_{rs}, and consider the implications for consistent aggregation of a knowledge of the distribution of those variables.

Consider the case in which $m = 1$; for example, let each household's consumption depend only on its income, which we shall write simply as x_s. We have seen earlier that if the functions f_s are taken to be polynomials, the use of moments as aggregates is useful (cf. above, p. 43).

Klein (1962, pp. 25–6) considers a simple case in which the functions f_s are quadratic, identical except for an additive constant. Then

$$y_s = a_s + bx_s + cx_s^2$$

$$y = \sum_{s=1}^{n} a_s + b \sum_{s=1}^{n} x_s + c \sum_{s=1}^{n} x_s^2$$

$$= a + bn\bar{x} + cn(\bar{x})^2 + cn\sigma_x^2$$

where $\bar{x}$ and σ_x^2 are respectively the mean and the variance of the variables x_s.

If the form of the functions f_s is not known, but the parameters of the distribution of the variables x_s are known, consistent aggregation may still be achieved, if the functions f_s are identical for all s, by using the parameters of the distribution as aggregates. Such aggregation will be desirable, however, to the extent that the number of such parameters is small, and their values are easy to calculate or estimate.

Let the density function $D(x)$ show the fraction of the total number of incomes lying between x and $x + dx$. Then (see de Wolff (1941)), if we write $\bar{x}$ for $1/n \sum_{s=1}^{n} x_s$, y for $\sum_{s=1}^{n} y_s$, and $f(x)$ for the consumption function, the same for all individuals

$$\int_0^\infty D(x)\, dx = 1; \qquad n \int_0^\infty D(x)\, dx = n;$$

$$\int_0^\infty xD(x)\, dx = \bar{x}; \qquad n \int_0^\infty f(x)D(x)\, dx = y.$$

De Wolff argues that if the density function $D(x)$ depends on a single parameter μ, so that y and $\bar{x}$ are both functions of μ, y will be a function of $\bar{x}$.[1] This is not true in general because there may be cases where $dy/d\mu \neq 0$ but $d\bar{x}/d\mu = 0$, so that two distinct values of y correspond to a single value of $\bar{x}$, and y is *not* a function of $\bar{x}$. It is true, however, that if the density function $D(x)$ depends on more than one parameter, y will not in general be a function of $\bar{x}$ (or of $\sum_{s=1}^{n} x_s$) alone.

Suppose, for example, that the density function $D(x)$ is normal or lognormal.[2] If the functions f_s are the same for all s, then y will depend, as does the density function, only on the mean (or sum) and the variance of the distribution. To take a specific example (see Prais and Houthakker (1955, pp. 13–14)), let

$$y_s = a + b \log x_s.$$

---

[1] Of course, if the function $f(x)$ is *linear* and the same for all individuals, total consumption y will, as we have seen, be a function of total income (or of $\bar{x}$) irrespective of the distribution of income.

[2] A set of variates is said to be lognormally distributed if the logarithms of its elements are normally distributed.

Then

$$y = \sum_{s=1}^{n} y_s = na + b \sum_{s=1}^{n} \log x_s$$

$$= na + bn \log x^*$$

where x^* is the geometric mean of the x_s's. We can express y in terms of the mean and variance of the x_s's themselves by using the following relationship between these parameters and the geometric mean, when the distribution is lognormal (see Aitchison and Brown (1957, p. 8))

$$\log x^* = 2 \log \bar{x} - \tfrac{1}{2} [\log (\bar{x}^2 + \sigma_x^2)]$$

where $\bar{x}$ is the arithmetic mean and σ_x^2 the variance of the x_s's.

4.

Let us now remove the assumption that $m = 1$, and represent the joint density function of the variables $x_{1s}, \cdots, x_{ms}$ by $D(x_1, \cdots, x_m)$, showing the fraction of the total number of points, n, lying in the hypercube defined by the points $x_1, \cdots, x_m$ and $x_1 + dx_1, \cdots, x_m + dx_m$. If we continue to assume that the functions f_s are identical, we have

$$y = n \int_{x_1} \int_{x_2} \cdots \int_{x_m} f(x_1, \cdots, x_m) D(x_1, \cdots, x_m) \, dx_m \cdots dx_2 \, dx_1 \quad (8.1)$$

We consider first the case of *independent* distributions. The meaning of this term is as follows. Let there be n_1 points whose coordinates for variables other than x_1 lie in the range R_1, between $(x_2', \cdots, x_m')$ and $(x_2' + dx_2, \cdots, x_m' + dx_m)$; let there be n_2 points whose coordinates for variables other than x_1 lie in the range R_2, between $(x_2'', \cdots, x_m'')$ and $(x_2'' + dx_2, \cdots, x_m'' + dx_m)$. Consider any range S of values of the variable x_1. If x_1 is distributed independently of the variables $x_2, \cdots, x_m$, then the proportion of the n_1 points of range R_1 whose x_1-coordinate lies in the range S will be the same as the proportion of the n_2 points of range R_2 whose x_1-coordinate lies in the range S. The joint density function can then be written as a product of two density functions, one for x_1 and one for all the other variables, as follows:

$$D(x_1, \cdots, x_m) = D_1(x_1) D'(x_2, \cdots, x_m)$$

and (8.1) becomes

$$y = n \int_{x_1} \int_{x_2} \cdots \int_{x_m} f(x_1, \cdots, x_m) D_1(x_1)$$

$$\cdot D'(x_2, \cdots, x_m) \, dx_m \cdots dx_2 \, dx_1 \quad (8.2)$$

The aggregate y may be written as a function of the parameters of the density function D_1 and of the joint density function D'. Among the parameters relating to D' will be some expressing correlations between the variables $x_2, \cdots, x_m$. But the independence of the distribution of x_1 implies that x_1 is uncorrelated with the other variables.

5.

An example which permits considerable simplification is to be found in Friedman (1957, pp. 18–19). Here $m = 4$, y is "permanent"consumption, x_1 is "permanent" income, x_2, x_3 and x_4 are interest rates, the ratio of non-human wealth to income, and factors influencing tastes. Friedman assumes that it is the ratio of y to x_1 that is a function of the other three variables

$$y_s = x_{1s} f(x_{2s}, x_{3s}, x_{4s}) \tag{8.3}$$

and that x_1 is distributed independently of the other three variables, so that

$$y = n \int_{x_4} \int_{x_3} \int_{x_2} \int_{x_1} x_1 f(x_2, x_3, x_4) D_1(x_1) D'(x_2, x_3, x_4)\ dx_1\ dx_2\ dx_3\ dx_4$$

$$= n \int_{x_4} \int_{x_3} \int_{x_2} \left[\int_{x_1} x_1 D_1(x_1)\ dx_1 \right] f(x_2, x_3, x_4) D'(x_2, x_3, x_4)\ dx_2\ dx_3\ dx_4$$

$$= n \int_{x_4} \int_{x_3} \int_{x_2} \bar{x}_1 f(x_2, x_3, x_4) D'(x_2, x_3, x_4)\ dx_2\ dx_3\ dx_4.$$

Note that the transition from the first line to the second, in which we collect terms involving only x_1 and integrate, is possible only because of the special form of the function (8.3).

Friedman concludes that

$$y = k x_1$$

where $x_1 = \sum_{s=1}^{n} x_{1s}$, and k depends on the distribution of the variables x_2, x_3 and x_4.

The inclusion of "factors influencing tastes" as a variable in Friedman's consumption function is an ingenious method of rendering palatable the assumption that the consumption functions of different individuals are the same. Malinvaud (1956a, pp. 122–3) uses this device to show that differences in tastes need not prevent consistent aggregation of a simple type. Let us write

$$y_s = f(x_{1s}, x_{2s})$$

where y_s is consumption, x_{1s} is income, and x_{2s} is a "taste" parameter. If the distributions of tastes and incomes are independent, we have

$$y = n \int_{x_2} \int_{x_1} f(x_1, x_2) D_1(x_1) D_2(x_2)\ dx_1\ dx_2.$$

As long as the parameters of the distribution of tastes do not change, y depends on the parameters of $D_1(x_1)$ alone. If the distribution of x_1 is normal or lognormal, y depends only on the mean and variance of incomes. To the extent that the variance of incomes remains unchanged, total consumption will be uniquely determined by total income.

6.

It emerges from the argument of this chapter that if we have knowledge of the joint distribution of the independent variables, and are willing to admit the parameters of this distribution as aggregates, consistent aggregation with $y = \sum_{s=1}^{n} y_s$ can be achieved. It may be possible, by introducing further independent variables, to avoid the difficulties presented by functions f_s which differ between individuals and firms.

A common assumption is that independent variables are normally or lognormally distributed. If two variables are *jointly* normally or lognormally distributed, their joint density function depends on their covariance, as well as their own means and variances.

We conclude with a list of the number of such aggregates required in various circumstances. It is assumed in each case that the functions $f_s(x_{1s}, \cdots, x_{ms})$ are identical.

Conditions	*Number of aggregates required*
(a) If the function f is linear	m (the means)
(b) If all the density functions are independent, and normal or lognormal	m (the means) m (the variances) —— **2m**
(c) If the variables are jointly normally or lognormally distributed, and there is no independence	m (the means) m (the variances σ_r^2) $m(m-1)/2$ (the covariances $\sigma_{qr}(q \neq r)$) ———— **(m² + 3m)/2**

The nature of the aggregate function $y = F(\ )$ will of course depend on the form of the function f. For further applications of the argument of this chapter see, for example, Tobin (1950) and Farrell (1954), and the references there cited.

CHAPTER 9

Intermediate Products and Aggregation Problems of Input-Output Analysis

1.

To the extent that the argument of earlier chapters has been applicable to production functions, the existence of intermediate products has been ignored; all outputs have been assumed to be final outputs and all inputs have been assumed to be original or non-produced inputs. We should, however, distinguish between the total output of a firm, Y_s, and its final output, y_s, which is the amount sold to final users (to consumers, to other firms on investment account, to government and to foreign buyers) rather than to other firms on current account. We therefore define

$$Y_s = y_s + \sum_{t=1}^{n} y_{st} = F_s(y_{1s}, \cdots, y_{ns}, x_{1s}, \cdots, x_{ms}) \qquad (9.1)$$

where y_{st} is the amount of the output of firm s used by firm t, and $x_{1s}, \cdots, x_{ms}$ are "original" inputs.

If we are interested in the production possibilities offered by a given set of original inputs, it is the quantities of *final* output available that concern us. Accordingly, we find the conditions for the optimal allocation of given quantities of original inputs by holding constant all final outputs y_s but one (say the first, y_1) and maximizing the value of the remaining final output y_1. For this purpose we form the Lagrange expression

$$\phi = F_1(y_{11}, \cdots, y_{n1}, x_{11}, \cdots, x_{m1}) - \sum_{s=1}^{n} y_{1s}$$

$$+ \sum_{s=2}^{n} \lambda_s \left\{ \bar{y}_s - \left[F_s(y_{1s}, \cdots, y_{ns}, x_{1s}, \cdots, x_{ms}) - \sum_{t=1}^{n} y_{st} \right] \right\}$$

$$+ \sum_{r=1}^{m} \mu_r \left(\bar{x}_r - \sum_{s=1}^{n} x_{rs} \right)$$

and set equal to zero the n^2 partial derivatives $\partial\phi/\partial y_{st}$ and the mn partial derivatives $\partial\phi/\partial x_{rs}$. The unknowns consist of the n^2 variables y_{st}, the mn variables x_{rs}, the $(n-1)$ Lagrange multipliers λ_s and the m Lagrange multipliers μ_r. This implies that we have $(m+n-1)$ degrees of freedom, which enable us to write down the transformation function relating the quantities of final output y_s and the quantities of original inputs x_r, exactly as in Chapter 6 (equation (6.2))

$$F(y_1, \cdots, y_n, x_1, \cdots, x_m) = 0.$$

But in the production functions $y_s = f_s(x_{1s}, \cdots, x_{ms})$ of Chapter 6, y_s was interpreted as final output and x_{rs} as original input. If intermediate products exist, what meaning can be given to such functions? The only way is to define a new set of variables x'_{rs}—the amount of the original input x_r used both directly *and* indirectly in the production of y_s. Then x'_{rs} is derived as follows. We take:

(a) the amount of x_r used *directly* in the production of the total output Y_s; that is, x_{rs} as it appears in equation (9.1) of the present chapter;

we *add*:

(b) the amounts of x_r used in the production of those intermediate products $y_{1s}, \cdots, y_{ns}$ which are used in the production of Y_s; for example, of the quantity x_{rt} used directly in the production of the final output Y_t, a proportion, y_{ts}/Y_t, may be regarded as going to produce y_s. Hence we add to x_{rs}:

$$\sum_{t=1}^{n} \frac{y_{ts}}{Y_t} x_{rt};$$

we *subtract*:

(c) the amounts of x_r embodied in the products supplied by firms to other firms. Thus we subtract:

$$\sum_{t=1}^{n} \frac{y_{st}}{Y_s} x_{rs}.$$

In short, we define:

$$x'_{rs} = x_{rs} + \sum_{t=1}^{n} \frac{y_{ts}}{Y_t} x_{rt} - \sum_{t=1}^{n} \frac{y_{st}}{Y_s} x_{rs}. \qquad (9.2)$$

Now since

$$\sum_{s=1}^{n} \sum_{t=1}^{n} \frac{y_{ts}}{Y_t} x_{rt} = \sum_{s=1}^{n} \sum_{t=1}^{n} \frac{y_{st}}{Y_s} x_{rs}$$

it may be seen that if we sum equations (9.2) over s we have, as we must

$$\sum_{s=1}^{n} x'_{rs} = \sum_{s=1}^{n} x_{rs} = x_r.$$

The production functions of Chapters 6 and 7, in their neglect of intermediate products, have implicity defined inputs as our variables x'_{rs}.[1] We recall Klein's argument, cited above (p. 45), that to investigate

---

[1] I would conjecture, however, that this definition of the variables x'_{rs} would create difficulties unless the functions F_s of equations (9.1) were homogeneous of degree one.

the conditions for consistent aggregation, on the assumption that the optimal conditions of production are satisfied, makes it difficult to trace the consequences of an innovation in a single industry. The argument just presented implies that if the individual production functions relate final outputs to original inputs (and Klein's production functions are of this kind), then an innovation in a single industry—a change in one of the total output functions F_s of equations (9.1)—will affect the *final* output functions $f_t(x'_{1t}, \cdots, x'_{mt})$ of all the firms that directly or indirectly sell to or buy from that industry. In this sense, an innovation which is confined to a single industry is almost inconceivable.

2.

The preceding discussion of intermediate products leads naturally to a consideration of input-output analysis, in which important aggregation problems arise. Each "elementary" industry is assumed to use the products of other industries in fixed proportions, so that, in the notation of equations (9.1)

$$y_{st} = a_{st} Y_t.$$

Samuelson (1951) has shown that this is a consequence of the satisfaction of the optimal conditions of production if (a) all the production functions F_s of (9.1) are homogeneous of degree one, (b) there is no joint production, (c) there is a single original input ($m = 1$).

We have, for each s and t

$$Y_s = y_s + \sum_{t=1}^{n} y_{st} = y_s + \sum_{t=1}^{n} a_{st} Y_t.$$

The n equations may be written as

$$\begin{bmatrix} 1 - a_{11} & \cdots & -a_{1s} & \cdots & -a_{1n} \\ \cdots & \cdots & \cdots & \cdots & \cdots \\ -a_{s1} & \cdots & 1 - a_{ss} & \cdots & -a_{sn} \\ \cdots & \cdots & \cdots & \cdots & \cdots \\ -a_{n1} & \cdots & -a_{ns} & \cdots & 1 - a_{nn} \end{bmatrix} \begin{bmatrix} Y_1 \\ \cdots \\ Y_s \\ \cdots \\ Y_n \end{bmatrix} = \begin{bmatrix} y_1 \\ \cdots \\ y_s \\ \cdots \\ y_n \end{bmatrix} \qquad (9.3)$$

or, briefly,

$$(I - A)Y = y$$

where I is the identity matrix, A is the matrix $((a_{st}))$, and Y and y are $n \times 1$ column vectors.

A question in keeping with the search for overall aggregates which has occupied us hitherto is: Can we aggregate the industries in such a way that we can write

$$y = (1 - a)Y$$

with $y = \sum_{i=1}^{n} w_s y_s$, $Y = \sum_{i=1}^{n} w_s Y_s$, and a constant?

Applying our usual procedure, we find that consistent aggregation requires both

$$dy = \sum_{s=1}^{n} w_s \, dy_s = \sum_{s=1}^{n} w_s \left(dY_s - \sum_{t=1}^{n} a_{st} \, dY_t \right)$$

$$= dY - \sum_{s=1}^{n} \sum_{t=1}^{n} w_s a_{st} \, dY_t$$

and

$$dy = (1 - a) \, dY = dY - a \sum_{t=1}^{n} w_t \, dY_t.$$

On the assumption that the variables Y_t may take on any values, it is necessary that for each t

$$\sum_{s=1}^{n} w_s a_{st} - a w_t = 0$$

or in matrix form,

$$
\begin{bmatrix}
a_{11} - a & \cdots & a_{s1} & \cdots & a_{n1} \\
\cdots & \cdots & \cdots & \cdots & \cdots \\
a_{1s} & \cdots & a_{ss} - a & \cdots & a_{ns} \\
\cdots & \cdots & \cdots & \cdots & \cdots \\
a_{1n} & \cdots & a_{sn} & \cdots & a_{nn} - a
\end{bmatrix}
\begin{bmatrix}
w_1 \\
\cdots \\
w_s \\
\cdots \\
w_n
\end{bmatrix}
=
\begin{bmatrix}
0 \\
\cdots \\
0 \\
\cdots \\
0
\end{bmatrix}
\tag{9.4}
$$

Now these are the equations defining the characteristic roots (a) and the characteristic vectors ($w_1, \cdots, w_n$) of the matrix

$$
\begin{bmatrix}
a_{11} & \cdots & a_{n1} \\
a_{1n} & \cdots & a_{nn}
\end{bmatrix}
\tag{9.5}
$$

This matrix appears on the left-hand side of equations (9.4), with a subtracted from each element of the main diagonal. The matrix (9.5) is the *transpose* of the matrix A of (9.3); a square matrix and its transpose have the same characteristic roots and vectors.

McManus (1956a, p. 34) points out: "Consistent aggregation into one big sector is always possible and in as many different ways as there are characteristic vectors which are not simply proportional to others." We should be dissatisfied, however, if some of the industry weights w_s were negative or zero. It can be shown that if there is no industry or group of m industries ($m < n$) that is completely self-sufficient,[2] then a characteristic vector of positive weights $w_1, \cdots, w_n$ will exist, "unique

[2] "Self-sufficiency" means that none of the output of any industry outside the group is used by the group. If the conditions stated in the text are satisfied, the matrix A is said to be "indecomposable."

except for a proportionality factor; the associated characteristic root[3] is real and positive, its value being greater than the absolute value of any other characteristic root" (McManus, *op. cit.* p. 35).

The interest of this "overall" aggregation problem in input-output analysis lies partly in the role of the set of positive weights just mentioned in recent theoretical work. These weights are the proportions which the outputs of different industries bear to each other when a general equilibrium system of the von Neumann type (with no joint production) is undergoing balanced growth; the associated characteristic root is the reciprocal of the maximum rate of growth: see Dorfman, Samuelson, and Solow (1958, pp. 381 ff.). The weights are also those used by Sraffa (1960) in the construction of his "standard commodity."

3.

A great deal of attention has been devoted to the proper grouping of industries into sectors in input-output analysis. This problem has aspects both of the grouping of variables discussed in Part II and of the aggregation of economic relations which has been our concern in Part III. Again we draw on the work of McManus (1956a).

The "elementary" industries, n in number, are to be grouped into m sectors, with n_r industries in the rth sector, so that $\sum_{r=1}^{m} n_r = n$. We wish therefore to be able to express the n equations (cf. equations (9.3)):

$$
\begin{bmatrix} y_{11} \\ \cdots \\ y_{r1} \\ \cdots \\ y_{rn_r} \\ \cdots \\ y_{mn_m} \end{bmatrix} = \begin{bmatrix} 1-a_{11 \cdot 11} & \cdots & -a_{11 \cdot r1} & \cdots & -a_{11 \cdot rn_r} & \cdots & -a_{11 \cdot mn_m} \\ \cdots & \cdots & \cdots & \cdots & \cdots & \cdots & \cdots \\ -a_{r1 \cdot 11} & \cdots & 1-a_{r1 \cdot r1} & \cdots & -a_{r1 \cdot rn_r} & \cdots & -a_{r1 \cdot mn_m} \\ \cdots & \cdots & \cdots & \cdots & \cdots & \cdots & \cdots \\ -a_{rn_r \cdot 11} & \cdots & -a_{rn_r \cdot r1} & \cdots & 1-a_{rn_r \cdot rn_r} & \cdots & -a_{rn_r \cdot mn_m} \\ \cdots & \cdots & \cdots & \cdots & \cdots & \cdots & \cdots \\ -a_{mn_m \cdot 11} & \cdots & -a_{mn_m \cdot r1} & \cdots & -a_{mn_m \cdot rn_r} & \cdots & 1-a_{mn_m \cdot mn_m} \end{bmatrix} \begin{bmatrix} Y_{11} \\ \cdots \\ Y_{r1} \\ \cdots \\ Y_{rn_r} \\ \cdots \\ Y_{mn_m} \end{bmatrix}
$$
(9.6)

in the form

$$
\begin{bmatrix} y_1 \\ \cdots \\ y_r \\ \cdots \\ y_m \end{bmatrix} = \begin{bmatrix} 1 - a_{11} & \cdots & -a_{1r} & \cdots & -a_{1m} \\ \cdots & \cdots & \cdots & \cdots & \cdots \\ -a_{r1} & \cdots & 1 - a_{rr} & \cdots & -a_{rm} \\ \cdots & \cdots & \cdots & \cdots & \cdots \\ -a_{m1} & \cdots & -a_{mr} & \cdots & 1 - a_{mm} \end{bmatrix} \begin{bmatrix} Y_1 \\ \cdots \\ Y_r \\ \cdots \\ Y_m \end{bmatrix}
$$
(9.7)

We assume that intrinsic aggregates exist in the form of simple sums, so that $Y_r = \sum_{k=1}^{n_r} Y_{rk}, y_r = \sum_{k=1}^{n_r} y_{rk}$. This is in keeping with the prac-

---

[3] That is, the value of a that satisfies equations (9.4) with this set of values of $w_1, \cdots, w_n$.

tice of measuring the variables Y_{rk} and y_{rk} in monetary units (pounds, dollars, etc.). If the conditions for consistent aggregation were satisfied for aggregates expressed as weighted sums, it would always be possible to redefine the units in which y_{rk} and Y_{rk} were measured, and to adjust the coefficients $a_{rk \cdot qi}$, in such a way as to make aggregation in terms of simple sums consistent.

For consistent aggregation we must have, for each r

$$dy_r = \sum_{k=1}^{n_r} dy_{rk} = \sum_{k=1}^{n_r} \left(dY_{rk} - \sum_{q=1}^{m} \sum_{j=1}^{n_q} a_{rk \cdot qi} \, dY_{qi} \right)$$

$$= dY_r - \sum_{k=1}^{n_r} \sum_{q=1}^{m} \sum_{j=1}^{n_q} a_{rk \cdot qi} \, dY_{qi}$$

and

$$dy_r = dY_r - \sum_{q=1}^{m} a_{rq} \, dY_q$$

$$= dY_r - \sum_{q=1}^{m} \sum_{j=1}^{n_q} a_{rq} \, dY_{qi}.$$

With the variables Y_{qi} free to take any values, we must have, for all q, r and $i, j = 1, \cdots, n_q$

$$a_{rq} = \sum_{k=1}^{n_r} a_{rk \cdot qi} = \sum_{k=1}^{n_r} a_{rk \cdot aj}. \tag{9.8}$$

These conditions may be illustrated by considering a sub-matrix of the matrix in (9.6); the rows are those corresponding to $x_{r1}, \cdots, x_{rn_r}$, and the columns correspond to $x_{q1}, \cdots, x_{qn_q}$. (If we chose $q = r$, the 1's in the matrix of (9.6) would be omitted from the diagonal elements of the sub-matrix).

$$
\begin{matrix}
-a_{r1 \cdot q1} & \cdots & -a_{r1 \cdot qi} & \cdots & -a_{r1 \cdot qn_q} \\
\cdots & \cdots & \cdots & \cdots & \cdots \\
-a_{rk \cdot q1} & \cdots & -a_{rk \cdot qi} & \cdots & -a_{rk \cdot qn_q} \\
\cdots & \cdots & \cdots & \cdots & \cdots \\
-a_{rn_r \cdot q1} & \cdots & -a_{rn_r \cdot qi} & \cdots & -a_{rn_r \cdot qn_q}
\end{matrix}
$$

Conditions (9.8) say simply that the column sums of any such sub-matrix must be equal.[4] If this is so, each such column sum is given the value a_{rq}, and consistent aggregation to (9.7) is possible (cf. Theil (1957) and Ara (1959)).

If we use an aggregated model in which intra-sector transactions are netted out (cf. Hatanaka (1952), McManus (1956b)), the aggregate

---

[4] If the aggregates Y_q, Y_r and y_q, y_r were *weighted* sums, it would be necessary to find sets of weights $w_{q1}, \cdots, w_{qn_q}$ and $w_{r1}, \cdots, w_{rn_r}$ such that the weighted column sums were proportional to the weights assigned to the columns.

coefficients a_{rr} disappear from the main diagonal of the matrix in (9.7); this diagonal then consists of 1's. Gross output must then be defined so as to exclude intra-sector transactions, viz:

$$Y_r^* = \sum_{k=1}^{n_r} \left(Y_{rk} - \sum_{j=1}^{n_r} a_{rk \cdot rj} Y_{rj} \right).$$

The coefficients a_{rq} in the aggregated matrix must also be changed—let us call their new values a_{rq}^*. The conditions for consistent aggregation may then be found, by an argument similar to that used above, to be

$$a_{rq}^* = \frac{\displaystyle\sum_{k=1}^{n_r} a_{rk \cdot qi}}{1 - \displaystyle\sum_{h=1}^{n_q} a_{qh \cdot qi}} = \frac{\displaystyle\sum_{k=1}^{n_r} a_{rk \cdot qi}}{1 - \displaystyle\sum_{h=1}^{n_q} a_{qh \cdot qi}} \tag{9.9}$$

These conditions are a shade less stringent than (9.8), since equations (9.8) imply (9.9), but the converse is not true (see McManus (1956b), pp. 486-7)).

It may also be verified that if consistent aggregation is possible, the coefficients of the "gross" matrix of (9.7) and the "net" matrix discussed here are related in the following way:

$$a_{rq}^* = \frac{a_{rq}}{1 - a_{qq}}.$$

4.

In considering reductions in the number of degrees of freedom, we shall find it very convenient to make use of matrix algebra; only the operations of multiplication and inversion of matrices will be needed. Again we draw on the work of McManus (1956a); see also Theil (1957).

The relationship between the aggregates y_r and the elementary final outputs y_{rk}, when $y_r = \sum_{k=1}^{n_r} y_{rk}$, can be expressed as follows:

$$y_a = \begin{bmatrix} y_1 \\ \cdots \\ y_r \\ \cdots \\ y_m \end{bmatrix} = \begin{bmatrix} \overbrace{1 \cdots 1}^{n_1} & \cdots & \overbrace{0 \cdots 0}^{n_r} & \cdots & \overbrace{0 \cdots 0}^{n_m} \\ 0 \cdots 0 & \cdots & 1 \cdots 1 & \cdots & 0 \cdots 0 \\ 0 \cdots 0 & \cdots & 0 \cdots 0 & \cdots & 1 \cdots 1 \end{bmatrix} \begin{bmatrix} y_{11} \\ \cdots \\ y_{1n_1} \\ \cdots \\ y_{r1} \\ \cdots \\ y_{rn_r} \\ \cdots \\ y_{m1} \\ \cdots \\ y_{mn_m} \end{bmatrix} = Wy \tag{9.10}$$

where y_a and y are column vectors of aggregated and elementary final outputs respectively, and W is the matrix consisting of 0's and 1's. Similarly

$$Y_a = WY \tag{9.11}$$

and from (9.6)

$$y = (I - A)Y. \tag{9.12}$$

We seek the conditions in which (9.12) can be aggregated to (9.7), or in matrix notation

$$y_a = (I - A_a)Y_a \tag{9.13}$$

where $(I - A_a)$ is the matrix of equations (9.7).

If the stringent conditions on the coefficients $a_{rk \cdot qi}$, discovered earlier to be necessary for consistent aggregation when the degrees of freedom are at a maximum, fail to be satisfied, we may nonetheless be helped by restrictions on the movements of the total outputs Y_{rk} or the final outputs y_{rk}.

Suppose that the total outputs $Y_{r1}, \cdots, Y_{rn_r}$ always move proportionally, and that this is true for all sectors. Then for all r and k, $Y_{rk} = h_{rk}Y_r$, and $\sum_{k=1}^{n_r} h_{rk} = 1$. This may be expressed as follows:

$$
Y =
\begin{bmatrix}
Y_{11} \\
\cdots \\
Y_{1n_1} \\
\vdots \\
\vdots \\
Y_{r1} \\
\vdots \\
Y_{rn_r} \\
\vdots \\
\vdots \\
Y_{m1} \\
\vdots \\
Y_{mn_m}
\end{bmatrix}
=
\begin{bmatrix}
h_{11} & 0 & 0 \\
\cdots & \cdots & \cdots \\
h_{1n_1} & 0 & 0 \\
& \cdots & \\
0 & h_{r1} & 0 \\
\cdots & \cdots & \cdots \\
0 & h_{rn_r} & 0 \\
& & \cdots \\
0 & 0 & h_{m1} \\
\cdots & \cdots & \cdots \\
0 & 0 & h_{mn_m}
\end{bmatrix}
\begin{bmatrix}
Y_1 \\
\cdots \\
Y_r \\
\cdots \\
Y_m
\end{bmatrix}
= HY_a \tag{9.14}
$$

From (9.10), (9.12) and (9.14)

$$y_a = Wy = W(I - A)Y = W(I - A)HY_a$$
$$= (WIH - WAH)Y_a = (WH - WAH)Y_a.$$

Since $\sum_{k=1}^{n_r} h_{rk} = 1$ for each r, it can be easily seen that $WH = I$. Hence

$$y_a = (I - WAH)Y_a \tag{9.15}$$

which is in the required form (9.13).

Suppose on the other hand that the final outputs y_{rk} in a given sector move proportionally, so that $y_{rk} = g_{rk}y_r$, with $\sum_{k=1}^{n_r} g_{rk} = 1$. Then a matrix G, similar in construction to the matrix H of (9.14), can be defined in such a way that

$$y = Gy_a. \tag{9.16}$$

Using (9.11), (9.12) and (9.16), and noting that the matrix $(I - A)$ in (9.12) can be inverted, we have

$$Y_a = WY = W(I - A)^{-1}y = W(I - A)^{-1}Gy_a$$

whence

$$y_a = [W(I - A)^{-1}G]^{-1}Y_a$$

as required.

It is possible that there are certain groups of industries whose final demands move together and certain groups whose total outputs move together. In this case, we may be able to aggregate (perhaps in more than one way) first on one basis and then on the other. We might aggregate the elementary total output and final output vectors Y and y to the vectors $\bar{Y}$ and $\bar{y}$ by means of the aggregating matrix $\bar{W}$. We might then aggregate $\bar{Y}$ and $\bar{y}$ to $\bar{\bar{Y}}$ and $\bar{\bar{y}}$ by means of the aggregating matrix $\bar{\bar{W}}$. Let the first aggregation be made possible by proportionality of total outputs, represented by the matrix H (cf. equation (9.14)); let the second aggregation be made possible by the proportionality of final outputs, represented by the matrix G (cf. equation (9.16)). Then we have

$$\bar{Y} = \bar{W}Y; \qquad \bar{y} = \bar{W}y$$
$$\bar{\bar{Y}} = \bar{\bar{W}}\bar{Y}; \qquad \bar{\bar{y}} = \bar{\bar{W}}\bar{y}$$
$$Y = H\bar{Y}; \qquad y = G\bar{y}.$$

After the first aggregation we have (cf. (9.15))

$$\bar{y} = (I - \bar{W}AH)\bar{Y}.$$

It follows that

$$\bar{\bar{Y}} = \bar{\bar{W}}\bar{Y} = \bar{\bar{W}}(I - \bar{W}AH)^{-1}\bar{y}$$
$$= \bar{\bar{W}}(I - \bar{W}AH)^{-1}G\bar{\bar{y}}$$

so that

$$\bar{\bar{y}} = [\bar{\bar{W}}(I - \bar{W}AH)^{-1}G]^{-1}\bar{\bar{Y}}$$

as required.

A treatment of the aggregation problem similar to, but less general than McManus's is that of Malinvaud (1956b). The study by Balderston and Whitin (1954) suffers, as McManus (1956a, p. 45) points out, from the weakness that, by contrast with pp. 73 ff above, it *begins* with the inverse of the matrix $(I - A)$: "but once the inverse is known, all the outputs are easily found, and in the original detail—and so the aggregation is unnecessary." The problem of *disaggregation*—of predicting the required total outputs of elementary industries from an aggregated model—is discussed by Fei (1956) and Malinvaud (1956a, pp. 113 ff., 139 ff.).

5.

We conclude this chapter, and Part III of the volume, with an interesting argument taken from a paper by Nataf (1953, pp. 46 ff.) to which we referred earlier. We assumed, until the present chapter, that production functions were differentiable and that iso-product surfaces were smoothly convex to the origin—in short, that the number of different processes available for the production of a given commodity was infinite. In the present chapter, it has been assumed that conditions are such that only one process is used in the production of each commodity (see above, p. 71).

Consider now an economy in which there are p distinct processes. A unit of the kth process, x_k, uses a_{rk} units of the rth input ($r = 1, \cdots , m$) and produces b_{sk} units of the sth output ($s = 1, \cdots , n$). The balance equations are: $a_r = \sum_{k=1}^{p} a_{rk}x_k$; $b_s = \sum_{k=1}^{p} b_{sk}x_k$.

Such a technology may be represented as follows:

$$\begin{bmatrix} a_{11} & \cdots & a_{1p} \\ \cdots & \cdots & \cdots \\ a_{m1} & \cdots & a_{mp} \\ b_{11} & \cdots & b_{1p} \\ \cdots & \cdots & \cdots \\ b_{n1} & \cdots & b_{np} \end{bmatrix} \begin{bmatrix} x_1 \\ \cdots \\ \cdots \\ \cdots \\ x_p \end{bmatrix} = \begin{bmatrix} a_1 \\ \cdots \\ a_m \\ b_1 \\ \cdots \\ b_n \end{bmatrix}$$

If the columns of the matrix are linearly independent, so that no column can be expressed as a linear combination of the others, and $p < m + n$, then p is the number of degrees of freedom in the system, and there are $m + n - p$ independent relationships among the variables $a_1, \cdots , a_m$, $b_1, \cdots , b_n$. The fewer the independent processes, the smaller is the number of macro-relations needed to describe the behaviour of the system. As an extreme example, if there were only one process, the value of any one of the a's or b's would determine the values of all the rest; the system would have only one degree of freedom.

If $p > m + n$, as in the case of smooth isoproduct surfaces where p is infinite, the number of degrees of freedom is $m + n$; as we saw in Chapter 6, this may be reduced to $(m + n - 1)$ if the optimal production conditions are satisfied. The problem of input-output analysis is one with $m = n$, with n distinct processes and therefore n degrees of freedom; see equations (9.3), where the values of $Y_1, \cdots , Y_n$ together uniquely determine the values of each of the variables $y_1, \cdots , y_n$.

Part IV

THE MEASUREMENT OF CAPITAL

CHAPTER 10

"Capital" in Models of Economic Growth

1.

In Part IV we consider some of the aggregation problems which arise in the construction of models of economic growth of the "neo-classical" variety (for example, Solow (1956a), Swan (1956), Meade (1961)). Such models contain an aggregate production function of the form

$$y = F(x_1, x_2, t) \tag{10.1}$$

where y is output, x_1 is capital, and x_2 is labour. The parameter t (time) is introduced in order to allow for shifts in the production function because of technical progress.

The aggregation problems implicit in the function (10.1) will be considered in three stages. In the first two stages which will occupy the rest of this chapter, we shall assume that technical progress is absent: $\partial F/\partial t = 0$. First of all, we shall ignore the special properties of capital which make its inclusion in an aggregate production function so troublesome; we shall treat x_1 and x_2 as if they were aggregates of current inputs. Secondly, we shall take account of the durability of capital and its declining efficiency as it grows older.

Thirdly, in Chapter 11, we shall consider the implications of technical progress for the measurability of capital.

2.

If we disregard the durability of the elements entering into the "capital" aggregate x_1, and assume that $\partial F/\partial t = 0$, the expression (10.1) is the result of aggregation of two types. The function F is the result of the aggregation of the production functions f_s of all firms (cf. Part III); the aggregates x_1 and x_2 are the result of the grouping of variables in those functions (cf. Part II). The basic functions are

$$y_s = f_s(x_{11 \cdot s}, \cdots, x_{1n_1 \cdot s}, x_{21 \cdot s}, \cdots, x_{2n_2 \cdot s}) \tag{10.2}$$

on the assumption that the numbers of different types of capital services and labour services are n_1 and n_2 respectively.[1]

On the usual assumption that the optimal conditions of production hold, and that x_{ir} is to be defined as $\sum_{s=1}^{n} x_{ir \cdot s}$ ($i = 1, 2; r = 1, \cdots, n_i$),

---

[1] We revert here to the assumption that inputs are "original" inputs; see above, pp. 69 ff. A further complication is introduced if a variable $x_{1r \cdot s}$ corresponds to a capital good of which several imperfectly substitutable models exist. An elaboration of the "surrogate production function" of Samuelson (1962) might be of assistance here.

we know from the results of Chapter 6 that if equations (10.2) are to be aggregated to

$$y = f(x_{11}, \cdots, x_{1n_1}, x_{21}, \cdots, x_{2n_2}) \tag{10.3}$$

the functions f_s must all be functions of one function which is homogeneous of degree one in the $(n_1 + n_2)$ inputs (see above, p. 53). Further reduction of (10.3) to (10.1) requires the existence of functions x_1 and x_2, each homogeneous of degree one, such that the functions (10.2) can be written as

$$y_s = \phi_s[x_1(x_{11 \cdot s}, \cdots, x_{1n_1 \cdot s}), x_2(x_{21 \cdot s}, \cdots, x_{2n_2 \cdot s})]$$

(See above, pp. 53–54.) The function F will then be homogeneous of degree one in the variables $x_1 = x_1(x_{11}, \cdots, x_{1n_1})$ and $x_2 = x_2(x_{21}, \cdots, x_{2n_2})$. All firms will use inputs in the same proportions.

These are of course extremely stringent conditions. In this chapter and the next we shall continue to assume that the only restrictions on degrees of freedom are those imposed by the optimal conditions of production, and draw the implications of the assumptions typically made concerning the functions and aggregates used in growth models. We postpone to Chapter 13 a consideration of possible constraints on the movements of the variables which may make such highly aggregated models more acceptable.

In the present context, however, note that even if we work with a less highly aggregated model in which p sectors are distinguished, so that (10.1) becomes

$$F(y_1, \cdots, y_p, x_1, x_2, t) = 0$$

it is still necessary that the two "grouping" functions $x_1(\ )$ and $x_2(\ )$ be the same for all firms in all sectors, though the sectors need not employ x_1 and x_2 in the same proportions.

3.

The aggregate production function F is typically assumed to be homogeneous of degree one in x_1 and x_2. It is reasonable to require that the aggregating function $y = y(y_1, y_2, \cdots, y_n)$ also be homogeneous of degree one,[2] so that a ten per cent increase in *each* output is measured as a ten per cent increase in aggregate output. Suppose then that x_1 and x_2 both increase by ten per cent, and that the whole of x_1 and x_2 is devoted to the production of a single commodity y_1. The two assumptions just stated imply (i) that y increases by ten per cent and (ii) that since $y(\lambda y_1, 0, \cdots, 0) = \lambda y(y_1, 0, \cdots, 0)$, y_1 must have increased by

---

[2] The function y will be considered in more detail in Chapter 13.

ten per cent. It follows that each of the individual functions f_s must be homogeneous of degree one in the inputs x_{s1} and x_{s2}. By the corollary to Theorem 10 (above, p. 50), we may therefore write

$$y = \sum_{s=1}^{n} c_s y_s.$$

If we wish, we may distinguish the outputs of capital goods (y_I) from those of consumption goods (y_{II}) as follows:

$$y = y_I + y_{II} = \sum_{s=1}^{i} c_s y_s + \sum_{u=k}^{n} c_u y_u. \tag{10.4}$$

4.

We have now shown that if the aggregate production function is homogeneous of degree one, consistent aggregation requires that the relative marginal costs of all goods (the coefficients c_s and c_u of (10.4)) must be constant, so that in competitive conditions their relative prices must be constant.

Now capital goods appear in growth models both as outputs and as inputs. If the relative prices of a set of inputs remain constant, then the ratios of their marginal products must remain constant in all firms. And if the ratios of their marginal products remain constant, and all production functions are functions of a single function which is homogeneous of degree one and has isoquants smoothly convex to the origin, then the ratios of the *quantities* of that set of inputs must remain constant.

Therefore the constancy of the relative prices of capital goods implies the constancy of their relative *quantities*. Net investment, therefore, must consist of the addition of a batch of capital goods in the same proportions as the stock that previously existed. We shall assume for simplicity that the different capital goods are produced in these same proportions and lose equal fractions of their value in a given time period, so that *gross* investment also adds capital goods in the fixed proportions.

Having stated these conditions, we shall henceforth disregard the existence of capital goods of different types (but not, of course, of different ages). It is not necessary for our present purposes to examine the consumption goods aggregate $y_{II} = \sum_{u=k}^{n} c_u y_u$,[3] but the relationship between the two aggregates y_I and y_{II} is of great importance. In the present chapter, since we assume no technical progress, we shall continue to assume that the relative prices of all commodities remain constant, so that it is of no consequence whether we take capital goods or consumption goods as numéraire. Solow (1956a) and Swan (1956) assume that

---

[3] But see Chapter 13 below.

relative prices of consumption goods and capital goods are unaffected even by technical progress. Meade (1961) permits the relative prices to vary, and we shall find it convenient, even in the absence of technical progress, to introduce into (10.4) the price of capital goods in terms of consumer goods, which we shall call p:

$$y = py_I + y_{II}. \tag{10.5}$$

We follow Meade in taking consumption goods as the numéraire.

5.

We now undertake the second stage of the investigation—a consideration of the problems raised by the durability of capital. The capital goods in existence at any time are of different ages, and their productivity declines with age. The capital stock available for use at time t, represented by the aggregate $x_1(t)$, is made up of capital goods produced in periods $t - 1$, $t - 2$, $\cdots$. Now if, as Swan (1956) assumes, capital goods last for ever with unimpaired efficiency, we may write

$$x_1(t) = \sum_{\theta=1}^{\infty} y_I(t - \theta).$$

Moreover, since there is no depreciation, there is no need to distinguish between gross and net output.

Gross output is defined as

$$y^g = py_I + y_{II}$$

where y_I is the amount of new capital goods produced. Net output is defined as gross output less depreciation; depreciation is the reduction, during the period under consideration, in the value of the stock of capital that existed at the beginning of the period.

It will be convenient to approach the problem of aggregating capital goods of different ages by analyzing the way in which depreciation may be calculated. Let us write the stock of capital at the beginning of period t in the form

$$x_1(t) = x_1(y_{I,t-1}, y_{I,t-2}, \cdots, y_{I,t-\theta}, \cdots).$$

On the assumption that both gross output y^g and net output y^n are functions of x_1 and x_2, we may draw on the analysis of a problem of Solow presented in Chapter 2 (pp. 11–12 above) for the conditions in which two outfits of capital goods of different age-distributions can represent the same quantity of capital. We can have

$$x_1' = x_1(y_{I,t-1}', \cdots, y_{I,t-\theta}', \cdots) = x_1'' = x_1(y_{I,t-1}'', \cdots, y_{I,t-\theta}'', \cdots)$$

only if

$$y^g = F^g(x_1', x_2) = F^g(x_1'', x_2)$$

and

$$y^n = F^n(x_1', x_2) = F^g(x_1', x_2) - D'$$
$$= F^n(x_1'', x_2) = F^g(x_1'', x_2) - D''$$

for all values of x_2, where the superscripts g and n represent "gross" and "net," and D' and D'' are the amounts by which the stocks x_1' and x_1'' depreciate. These conditions imply that D' and D'' must be equal.

Now both gross and net output (cf. equation (10.5)) are measured in terms of current consumption goods. It follows that depreciation—the loss in value of the stock of capital resulting from the production of y^g—is also measured in terms of current consumption goods. The lost value consists of a potential yield of future consumption goods, which can be translated into current consumption goods only by the use of a discount factor. But the two streams of potential yields D' and D'' would in general be equal in value at only one rate of discount, and different at all others. In order to discover, therefore, whether the two stocks of capital x_1' and x_1'' represent equal quantities of capital, it is necessary to know the rate of discount or the rate of interest. But in the growth models under discussion, it is claimed that the rate of interest is determined in part by the quantity of capital. This circularity, pointed out by Mrs. Robinson (1954) and Kaldor (1956), can be avoided only by means of special assumptions.

The necessary assumptions may be discovered as follows. Let the current value, somehow defined, of the capital goods produced in period $(t - \theta)$ be written as $f_\theta(y_{I,t-\theta})$. Then

$$x_1(t) = \sum_{\theta=1}^{\infty} f_\theta(y_{I,t-\theta}).$$

Let the loss in value during period t of the capital goods produced in period $(t - \theta)$, a fraction d_θ of its current value, be $d_\theta \cdot f_\theta(y_{I,t-\theta})$. But if we are to escape from the vicious circle involving the rate of interest, total depreciation must be independent of the age-structure of the stock of capital, and must depend only on its quantity $x_1(t)$. Hence, if we define the function $D(x_1)$ as the depreciation occurring in the stock of capital, and use primes for differentiation, we have

$$D[x_1(t)] = D\left[\sum_{\theta=1}^{\infty} f_\theta(y_{I,t-\theta})\right] = \sum_{\theta=1}^{\infty} d_\theta \cdot f_\theta(y_{I,t-\theta})$$

so that

$$D' \sum_{\theta=1}^{\infty} f_\theta' \, dy_{I,t-\theta} = \sum_{\theta=1}^{\infty} d_\theta \cdot f_\theta' \, dy_{I,t-\theta}.$$

Since all age-structures of the capital stock are admissible, it follows that

$$D' = d_1 = d_2 = \cdots = d_\theta = \cdots.$$

Depreciation must reduce the value of capital goods of all ages in the same proportion.

The production function can be defined in such a way that the brand-new capital goods produced in period $(t - 1)$ are counted in the capital aggregate $x_1(t)$ at the value $y_{I, t-1}$. The depreciation occurring during the period $(t - 1)$ reduced in the ratio δ_{t-1} the values of capital goods of all ages existing at the beginning of period $(t - 1)$. Hence

$$x_1(t) = y_{I, t-1} + \delta_{t-1} y_{I, t-2} + \delta_{t-1} \delta_{t-2} y_{I, t-3} + \cdots$$
$$+ \delta_{t-1} \delta_{t-2} \cdots \delta_{t-\theta} y_{I, t-\theta-1} + \cdots.$$

Thus as time passes old capital goods become the equivalent of an ever-decreasing fraction of brand-new capital goods.

The rate at which the capital stock depreciates during period t may depend on the amount of labour x_2 cooperating with capital. Unless we assume that the amount of labour employed with a unit of capital is rigidly fixed, therefore, it is not necessary that the proportional decline in the value of the capital stock should be the same in every period.[4] (The foregoing argument does imply, however, that no capital goods, however old, wear out completely unless the whole capital stock wears out completely.)

6.

It may be argued that to treat gross and net outputs as a function of labour and the *stock* of capital alone is unduly restrictive: "it seems to imply that we recognize depreciation due to the passage of time but deny the existence of depreciation due to service or to 'user cost.' " (Samuelson (1961, p. 34)). The variable x_1 in (10.1) is properly regarded as a *flow* of capital services, which may be increased by using a given *stock* of capital more intensively. The intensity of use may be measured simply by the rate of depreciation δ. It follows that gross output is not strictly a function of x_1 and x_2 alone. This difficulty may be overcome by following Samuelson's suggestion (*loc. cit.*) that for given values of x_1 and x_2 we suppose the rate of depreciation δ to be selected in such a way that net output is maximized. Thus

$$y^n = \underset{\delta}{\mathrm{Max}} \; [y^g(x_1, x_2, \delta) - \delta \cdot x_1].$$

---

[4] The assumption of fixed proportions of labour and capital is implicit in an argument presented elsewhere, (Green (1962)), in which it is shown that the proportional decline must be the same in every period.

Such a procedure implies that y^n, y^g and δ all depend on x_1 and x_2 alone.

If the gross and net output functions thus defined are both homogeneous of degree one in x_1 and x_2, then the depreciation rate δ must be homogeneous of degree zero in x_1 and x_2; it will depend only on the *ratio* of x_1 and x_2. This may be seen as follows:

$$F^g(x_1, x_2) - F^n(x_1, x_2) = x_1 \cdot \delta(x_1, x_2)$$

$$F^g(\lambda x_1, \lambda x_2) - F^n(\lambda x_1, \lambda x_2) = \lambda[x_1 \cdot \delta(x_1, x_2)] = \delta(x_1, x_2) \cdot \lambda x_1.$$

But in the same way

$$F^g(\lambda x_1, \lambda x_2) - F^n(\lambda x_1, \lambda x_2) = \lambda x_1 \cdot \delta(\lambda x_1, \lambda x_2).$$

Hence

$$\delta(x_1, x_2) = \delta(\lambda x_1, \lambda x_2)$$

as required.[5]

Three brief comments on the problem of depreciation are suggested by the results of this chapter. In the first place, we have assumed that the rate of depreciation δ is the same for all types of capital goods. We are at liberty, of course, to distinguish a number of groups of capital goods, depreciating at different rates.

Secondly, it is an implication of our aggregation conditions that no capital goods are ever discarded: their value never falls to zero, no matter what their age. Now in the optimal world envisaged here, if capital equipment is in fact discarded, it must be because its scrap value comes to exceed its value in its existing form. The scrap value will reflect its productivity in the construction of new equipment. Hence if the value of a piece of old equipment is written down to zero, in apparent violation of our aggregation conditions, it could be argued that both depreciation and gross investment (because of the availability of the scrap) would be higher, and net investment would be just the same, as if the old capital goods had been regarded as continuing to depreciate at the same rate as the rest of the capital stock.

Thirdly, measurement by original cost without deducting depreciation, one of the three methods for valuing the capital stock mentioned by Denison (1957) in a well-known article, might appear at first sight to circumvent the "circularity" encountered earlier in this chapter. If depreciation is not deducted, the problem of an intrusive discount factor does not arise. This is, of course, an illusion. A piece of capital equipment disappears from the capital stock all at once, if this method

---

[5] The statement in a paper by the author (Green (1960, p. 62)) that in general the gross and net output functions will not *both* be homogeneous of degree one is seen, on the basis of the present argument, to have no foundation.

is used, in the year in which it is discarded; depreciation is deducted in the final year of the equipment's life, rather than spread over its life. Such a procedure will give a misleading picture of the value of the stock of capital at any one time, since as Domar (1953) pointed out in a classic article, the value of depreciation in a given year will in general differ from the value of discards during that year if the stock of capital is growing. The difference will fail to exist only if depreciation takes the form of the disappearance each year of a certain fraction of the capital stock, with equipment of all ages affected in the same way; this is precisely the condition derived above. See also Meade (1961).

7.

Before concluding this chapter, we feel bound to comment on the appropriateness of equation (10.5) as a measure of real output. If a measure of real output is to be of significance, its value should bear some relationship to a community's well-being. This general problem will be considered in Chapter 13; we wish here to consider only the significance of valuing the output of investment goods in terms of current consumption goods.

First of all, since it is net output which is of interest, let us rewrite (10.5) as

$$y^* = p(y_I - \delta \cdot x_1) + y_{II} \qquad (10.6)$$

where of course $y_I - \delta \cdot x_1$ is the volume of net investment. Let us accept for the purposes of this discussion that welfare increases as y_{II}, the output of consumption goods, increases. In what sense, if any, can it be argued that equal increases in y_{II} and $p(y_I - \delta \cdot x_1)$ make equal contributions to welfare, as (10.6) implies?

A standard argument would be that the value of investment in terms of current consumption is found by taking the volume of investment, multiplying by the marginal productivity of investment in terms of future consumption of goods, and discounting these future yields at the appropriate rates of interest. But in equilibrium the discounted value of future yields of consumption goods is precisely equal to the price of capital goods in terms of consumption goods (see, for example, Gordon (1961, p. 954n)). It would appear, therefore, that multiplication of the volume of investment by p, as in (10.6), is what is required.

But this is not really satisfactory, as a persuasive argument by Samuelson (1961, pp. 44 ff.) shows. Consider two economies A and B. It is quite possible for the marginal productivity of capital goods to be higher in A than in B, but for the rate of interest to be similarly higher in A, so that the price of capital goods in terms of consumption goods is the same in the two economies. Any point on the line CD in Fig. 3

represents the same value of y'' in both economy A and economy B. But since the marginal productivity of capital goods is higher in A, if the same amount y_{II} is consumed out of the same net output in the two economies, the remaining output of investment goods will permit a greater increase in consumption in future periods in economy A than in economy B. The possibilities of additional consumption now and in the future represented by these equal values of investment in the two economies are shown by the lines A and B in Fig. 4. It is hard to escape the conclusion that for any value of y'', however it may be allocated between consumption and investment, economy A is better off than economy B.

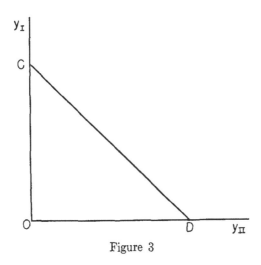

Figure 3

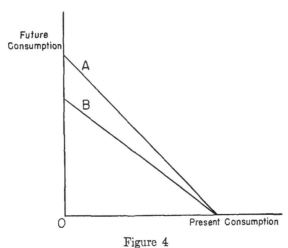

Figure 4

Samuelson concludes that welfare measurement in terms of income is difficult and fundamentally uninteresting, and that some sort of wealth measurement, though even more difficult to come by, is what we need. This is an important argument. Most growth theorists do in fact measure output by means of a formula like (10.6), though Mrs. Robinson (1956) was clearly aware of the difficulty Samuelson raises when she wrote: "an over-all comparison of output per man can properly be made only between economies in each of which there is no net investment" (p. 117).

What our formula (10.6) does measure is the level of consumption which could be enjoyed in perpetuity if there were no net investment—if the present stock of capital, the present flow of labour services, and the present techniques were maintained.[6] This conforms to the spirit of the definition of income given some time ago by Hicks (1946, Ch. XIV), and in view of the difficulty of arriving at an estimate of Samuelson's "wealth," it is perhaps the best that can be hoped for.

[6] This interpretation would not be possible unless the production possibility surfaces were hyperplanes. If they had the usual shape (see the accompanying diagram) output as measured would be OB, while the maximum output of consumption goods would be only OA.

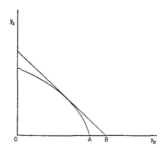

CHAPTER 11

Technical Progress and Capital Measurement

1.

In this chapter we shall be concerned with technical progress, to the extent that it affects the aggregation problems discussed in the previous chapter.

Since our concern is primarily with the measurement of capital, we shall discuss only briefly quality changes in consumer goods. In Chapter 10 we were able to aggregate the outputs of consumer goods by means of the formula $y_{II} = \sum_{u=k}^{n} c_u y_u$, on the assumption that their relative prices were constant. If technical progress alters the relative prices of consumption goods, a comparison of two sets of outputs of consumption goods is possible only if the aggregating function $y_{II}(y_k, \cdots, y_n)$ is specified; this will be discussed in Chapter 13.

There is, however, a further problem: technical progress may change the nature of consumption goods, or lead to the introduction of new ones. How are new or different goods to be introduced into the aggregate y_{II}? One suggestion is that commodities of a particular type should be identified by certain characteristics (e.g., the liquid volume and alcohol volume of beer, or the length, weight and horse-power of automobiles; see Stone (1956, Ch. IV and references), Adelman and Griliches (1961)). Changes in quality, or the introduction of new commodities, would then be regarded as changing the quantities of these characteristics, which would become the new "elementary commodities."

If quality changes occur, but we wish to continue to aggregate consumption goods by the formula $y_{II} = \sum_{u=k}^{n} c_u y_u$, we must assume that the relative prices of the "elementary commodities" remain unchanged. This assumption will permit us to continue to disregard the existence of different types of consumption goods.

We wish to permit the prices of capital goods in terms of consumption goods to change. We shall, however, continue to disregard the existence of different types of capital goods, assuming as in the case of consumption goods that the relative prices of different types (or different "characteristics") remain unchanged. Our main concern, as in the previous chapter, will be the aggregation of capital goods of different *ages*.

2.

If the quantities of old and new capital goods are to be aggregated, and the sum of their values is to be entered in a production function, then the relative values of old and new capital goods as measured by the aggregate must reflect their relative contributions to production. The basis for the construction of an index of capital goods must be productivity.

Technical progress takes a number of forms. The nature of capital goods changes; the skills of the labour force change; the methods of combining capital and labour change. We found in Chapter 2 that if capital goods of different types (or different ages, or different models) are to be included in a single index of capital, it is necessary that the marginal rate of substitution between them be independent of the quantity (or skill) of labour used with them. If our aggregate is to be a *sum*, the marginal rate of substitution must be constant (the two types of capital goods must be perfect substitutes). We must imagine that we could take a brand-new machine of the latest model, and discover how many brand-new machines of an older model are necessary, with the same quantity of current labour, with current skills, to produce the same output. Now we must imagine that the brand-new machine of the latest model was available when the older model was brand-new, and ask how many machines of the older model were necessary, with a given quantity of labour having the skills of that time, to produce the same output as the latest model. If, and only if, the number of machines of the old model needed to match a new model is the same in each case, we have a basis for an index of capital goods. Taking a brand-new machine of any one age as an "efficiency unit," we may then express brand-new machines of all ages in terms of such units. The value in efficiency units of the current stock of capital is then obtained by deducting depreciation, in the manner indicated in the preceding chapter.

3.

If we are agreed that capital goods of different ages must be compared, for the purposes of the aggregate production function, on the basis of their productivity, then measurement in terms of *cost* must be regarded with suspicion. Let us suppose that an old machine, when it was new, cost as much to produce as a unit of consumption goods. And let us suppose that a brand-new machine costs as much to produce now as a unit of consumption goods.[1] Assume that the brand-new machine represents twice as many "efficiency units" of capital as the old machine. It would be quite inconsistent with the argument of this chapter to say that the two machines represent the same quantity or value of capital because their costs are the same. We should say rather that the new model represents twice as much capital as the old model (when it was brand-new), and that the price of capital goods in terms of consumer's goods has fallen by one-half.

[1] We assume that units of consumption goods can be equated over time.

4.

As Goldsmith (1961, p. 445) points out, the valuation of the stock of capital at any time requires data of three kinds:

(a) The value of the stock of capital at a benchmark date: such a valuation can in practice be obtained at infrequent intervals, and may be based on market values at that time (if obtainable), or on the cost of replacement of the stock in its condition at that time.

(b) An estimate of rates of depreciation through use: ideally, as we saw in Chapter 10, the rate in any one period would be the same for all capital goods of all ages.

(c) A price-index of capital goods: ideally, this index would measure the change in the cost of an "efficiency unit" of capital goods as defined above. On the difficulties of constructing and interpreting such an index, see Gordon (1961).

To estimate the value of the capital stock in any year, we add to the pre-existing stock the value of gross investment deflated by the price index of capital goods. If this index has the value of 100 in the benchmark year, deflation ideally yields a measure of gross investment in "efficiency units"; the efficiency unit is one dollar's worth of capital in the bench-mark year. We deduct a certain fraction of the value of the pre-existing stock for depreciation through use. Consistency may be checked periodically by comparing the results of this procedure with a direct evaluation of the capital stock (by market value or replacement cost) deflated by the capital goods price index.

If a value of x_1 obtained in this way is inserted in the aggregate production function (10.1), the value of y corresponding to given values of x_1 and x_2 may shift over time for two reasons. (i) If the quality and skills of the labour force improve, but labour, x_2, is measured in man-hours, the function F will change because a given quantity of labour so measured will be more productive. This source of shift could be eliminated by devising an index of labour inputs measured in "efficiency units"; the construction of such an index would involve problems similar to some of those we have encountered in our discussion of a capital index. (ii) The residual shift in the function F is typically identified, in neo-classical growth models, as "technical progress," which increases the output obtainable from given quantities of capital and labour.

5.

We conclude this chapter with three comments on points raised in other discussions of capital measurement.

First, it must be stressed that if capital can be measured in efficiency units as suggested above, then it is quite consistent to speak of technical progress as increasing the marginal productivity of a given quantity of capital. We emphasize that measurement of capital in efficiency units does *not* imply that machine A represents twice as much capital as machine B if it produces twice as much output with a given quantity of labour (cf. Hicks's interpretation of his own "forward-looking" measure (1961, p. 30) and Kaldor's comment (1961, p. 304 *infra*)). It implies that machine A represents twice as much capital as machine B if, with a given quantity of labour, one A-machine produces the same output as two B-machines; this is quite a different matter. There is no reason why the marginal productivity of capital, measured in terms of B-machine equivalents or "efficiency units," can not increase.

Secondly, there is a way of regarding technical progress which in effect equates it with a falling price of capital goods in terms of consumption goods. This is the treatment of technical progress as wholly "embodied" in new capital goods; see, for example, Solow (1962). With "disembodied" technical progress, which we have so far assumed, the new skills and methods, of which "technical progress" consists, will affect in the same proportion the marginal productivity of all capital goods, whatever their age. If technical progress is wholly embodied in new capital goods, however, the new skills and methods are applied to new capital goods only: older equipment continues to be used in the old ways. It *would* be true in this case that technical progress would be reflected in an increase in the quantity of capital x_1, rather than

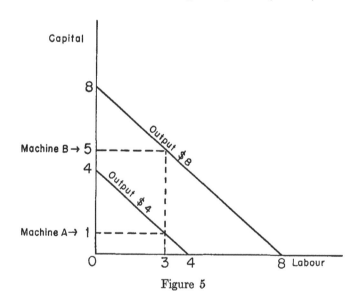

Figure 5

in a shift of the function F; the shift parameter t in the expression $F(x_1, x_2, t)$ would be absorbed in the capital aggregate x_1; see Solow, *op. cit.*

As Solow points out, he has himself "worked both sides of the street in different papers"; compare Solow (1962) with Solow (1957). He believes the truth to lie somewhere between the "embodied" and "disembodied" positions. It is usual in neo-classical growth models, however, to treat technical progress as "disembodied".[2]

Thirdly, we draw attention to a hypothetical problem posed by Denison (1957) in an article referred to earlier. He asks for a comparison of the relative quantities of capital represented by two machines. Three men, working with machine A, receive $1 each in wages and produce output worth $4. Machine B, a newer model, costs the same amount to produce as machine A, but enables the same three men to produce output worth $8. Now if we take the view that technical progress is "disembodied," so that the production function may have shifted between the periods in which machine A and machine B became available, we do not have sufficient information to compare the two machines in terms of efficiency units. We have one point on each of two isoquants, and the two isoquants belong to different families. The type of information needed in order to answer Denison's question has been specified on page 92 above.

If we assume that technical progress is "embodied" wholly in new capital goods, the production function does not shift, and the two isoquants, on each of which we know a single point, belong to the same family. If we further assume that the isoquants are straight lines, so that units of capital and labour are perfect substitutes, we obtain one of the answers proposed by Denison to his own question, namely, that machine B represents five times as much capital as machine A. (See Fig. 5.) If we do not assume that isoquants are straight lines, we again have insufficient information.

---

[2] It was my intention, in my paper on growth models, Green (1960), to treat technical progress as "disembodied." I made, however, what now seem to me to be two errors. In the first place, I took, as a unit of capital, the amount which now costs as much to produce as a unit of consumption goods. But capital should be measured in "efficiency units," and it will be only by a strange coincidence that the cost of an efficiency unit of capital in terms of consumption goods will remain constant over time. Secondly, it was quite wrong to write down the value of old capital because of obsolescence, as well as depreciation through use. If a brand-new machine of a particular vintage is selected as an efficiency unit, a particular machine of that vintage may decline in value through use. But to write its value down also because of obsolescence is to change the units in which capital is measured.

This correction implies that the discount factor in equation (3) of that work (p. 62) should be changed from $(r + u + a)$ to $(r + u)$. A number of changes are necessitated in the subsequent argument; in particular in equations (5), (5'), (8), (9) and (10), and in the first complete paragraphs of p. 72.

6.

We summarize briefly the results of Part IV. An aggregate production function displaying constant returns to scale implies strictly that the production functions for all commodities are subject to constant returns to scale, and that all firms use inputs in the same proportions. The aggregation of capital goods of all ages into a single index implies that all capital goods, whatever their age, lose in any one period equal fractions of their values through depreciation.

The use of the concept of "aggregate output" involves a cavalier treatment of time-preference and of quality changes in consumer goods. Waiving these difficulties, "efficiency units" of capital in general can be defined if (a) the marginal rate of substitution between old and new capital goods of a given type is constant, irrespective of the quantity and skill of cooperating labour, and (b) the cost in terms of consumers' goods of "efficiency units" of different types of capital goods change in the same proportion. Technical progress may be regarded *either* as increasing the *productivity* of given quantities of capital and labour *or* as increasing, by definition, the *quantity* of capital alone.

The conditions necessary for the consistency of the type of aggregation implicit in neo-classical growth models are, of course, impossible of realization. We would point out, however, that even if models using a number of sectors are used instead, problems of a similar type and severity arise within each sector. Our conditions are so stringent because we have permitted no limitations on the degrees of freedom of the system beyond those imposed by the optimal conditions of production.

In fact, further limitations will usually exist, both for growth models and for the other models discussed in this volume. A decision on the acceptability of a particular type and degree of aggregation is complex, depending as it does on considerations of an economic and statistical nature and on the purposes of the user of the model. In Part V we try to indicate some of the factors which must be taken into account in reaching a decision as to the appropriate aggregation procedures.

Part V

INCONSISTENT AGGREGATION

CHAPTER 12

Aggregation and Estimation

1.

Our discussion of aggregation to this point has been concerned exclusively with strict conditions for consistent aggregation. The statistical aspects of the problem have been disregarded. This disregard, in what purports to be an introductory survey of the literature, may perhaps be justified by a similar emphasis in the bulk of the contributions to the field.

But a question of fundamental importance, which must have occurred to any reader of the foregoing chapters, is the following. Since the conditions for consistent aggregation are always stringent, how serious are the inconsistencies which must inevitably result in practice from aggregation?

This question suggests the view, stressed by many authors, including Hood (1952), Hurwicz (1952), Malinvaud (1956a, pp. 132 ff.) and Theil (1954), that the problem of the appropriate type and degree of aggregation belongs to the field of statistical decision theory. As Malinvaud points out, in a model of which the purpose is to predict, decisions as to (a) the nature of the macro-theory (i.e., the relationships among the aggregates) to be selected, (b) the method of statistical estimation to be used, and (c) the aggregation procedures to be adopted, are all interrelated. The purposes of the investigator are of course paramount, and he must weigh the errors he may believe likely to result from a high degree of aggregation against the cost of using a disaggregated model.

In this chapter we shall illustrate these points by discussing contributions dealing with aggregation bias in the estimation of parameters, and with the accuracy of predictions of aggregated and disaggregated models. In Chapter 13 we shall pick up the threads of Chapters 10 and 11, discussing some of the inconsistencies of aggregation involved in the use of aggregate production functions.

2.

We found in Chapter 5 that in the case where

$$y_s = f_s(x_{1s}, \cdots, x_{ms}) \tag{12.1}$$

consistent aggregation to $y = f(x_1, \cdots, x_m)$, with $y = \sum_{s=1}^{n} y_s$ and $x_r = \sum_{s=1}^{n} x_{rs}$ is possible only if the functions f_s are of the form

$$y_s = a_s + \sum_{r=1}^{m} b_r x_{rs}.$$

For the purpose of defining aggregation bias, let us retain the assumption of linearity, but allow the coefficients b_{rs} in the functions

$$y_s = a_s + \sum_{r=1}^{m} b_{rs}x_{rs}$$

to differ between individuals. Let us also assume that these relationships do not hold exactly, but that in each time period under consideration, y_s differs from the value assigned by the equation by an "error" term u_s. Thus

$$y_s(t) = a_s + \sum_{r=1}^{m} b_{rs}x_{rs}(t) + u_s(t). \tag{12.2}$$

We also assume that the variables x_{rs} are related to the aggregates $x_1, \cdots, x_m$ by linear equations, also subject to error terms

$$x_{rs}(t) = \alpha_{rs} + \sum_{q=1}^{m} \beta_{rs \cdot q}x_q(t) + v_{rs}(t). \tag{12.3}$$

Since $\sum_{s=1}^{n} x_{rs} = x_r$, it follows that for all r, and in all time-periods t

$$\sum_{s=1}^{n} \alpha_{rs} = \sum_{s=1}^{n} v_{rs}(t) = 0; \ \sum_{s=1}^{n} \beta_{rs \cdot q} = 1 \text{ if } r = q; \ =0 \text{ if } r \neq q. \tag{12.4}$$

From (12.2) and (12.3)

$$y(t) = \sum_{s=1}^{n} y_s(t) = \sum_{s=1}^{n} \left(a_s + \sum_{r=1}^{m} b_{rs}\alpha_{rs} \right)$$
$$+ \sum_{q=1}^{m} \left[\sum_{s=1}^{m} \sum_{r=1}^{m} b_{rs}\beta_{rs \cdot q}x_q(t) \right] + \sum_{s=1}^{n} \left[u_s(t) + \sum_{r=1}^{m} b_{rs}v_{rs}(t) \right]. \tag{12.5}$$

Hence, as Theil points out [(1954, pp. 14, 111); see also Allen (1956, Ch. 20)], the parameters and the error term of the aggregate equation

$$y(t) = a + \sum_{q=1}^{m} b_q x_q(t) + u(t) \tag{12.6}$$

will have the following properties:

(1) $a = \sum_{s=1}^{n} a_s + \sum_{s=1}^{n} \sum_{r=1}^{m} b_{rs}\alpha_{rs}$: the constant term in (12.6) is the sum of the corresponding constant terms a_s of the individual equations (12.2), plus a term involving the "non-corresponding" terms b_{rs}, which are the coefficients of the variables x_{rs} in equations (12.2);

(2) $b_q = \sum_{s=1}^{n} \sum_{r=1}^{m} b_{rs}\beta_{rs \cdot q} = (1/n) \sum_{s=1}^{n} b_{qs} + \sum_{s=1}^{n} (\beta_{qs \cdot q} - (1/n))b_{qs} + \sum_{s=1}^{n} \sum_{r \neq q}^{m} b_{rs}\beta_{rs \cdot q}$: the coefficient of $x_q(t)$ in (12.6) is the arithmetic mean of the corresponding coefficients b_{qs}, plus a weighted arithmetic mean of the coefficients b_{qs}, plus a sum of weighted arithmetic means of the "non-corresponding" coefficients $b_{rs}(r \neq q)$;

(3) $u(t) = \sum_{s=1}^{n} u_s(t) + \sum_{s=1}^{n} \sum_{r=1}^{m} b_{rs} v_{rs}(t)$: the error term in (12.6) is the sum of the error terms of the individual equations (12.2), plus a weighted sum of the "non-corresponding" parameters b_{rs}.

All terms other than $\sum_{s=1}^{n} a_s$, $(1/n) \sum_{s=1}^{n} b_{qs}$ and $\sum_{s=1}^{n} u_s(t)$ are defined as forms of "aggregation bias." It can easily be shown, by making use of the conditions (12.4), that all the bias terms can be represented in terms of covariances. For example

$$\sum_{s=1}^{n} (b_{rs} - \bar{b}_r)(\alpha_{rs} - \bar{\alpha}_r) = \sum_{s=1}^{n} (b_{rs} - \bar{b}_r)\alpha_{rs} = \sum_{s=1}^{n} b_{rs}\alpha_{rs}$$

since by (12.4), $\sum_{s=1}^{n}\alpha_{rs} = 0$. ($\bar{\alpha}_r$ and $\bar{b}_r$ are arithmetic means). Hence we may write

$$a = \sum_{s=1}^{n} a_s + n \sum_{r=1}^{m} \mathrm{cov}\,(b_{rs}, \alpha_{rs})$$

$$b_q = \frac{1}{n} \sum_{s=1}^{n} b_{qs} + n \sum_{r=1}^{m} \mathrm{cov}\,(b_{rs}, \beta_{rs \cdot q}) \qquad (12.7)$$

$$u(t) = \sum_{s=1}^{n} u_s(t) + n \sum_{r=1}^{m} \mathrm{cov}\,(b_{rs}, v_{rs}(t))$$

Some of the cases considered in earlier chapters may be re-interpreted in the light of these expressions.

(i) If in equations (12.2) $b_{r1} = b_{r2} = \cdots = b_{rn}$ for each r, then all the covariances of equations (12.7) vanish. There is no aggregation bias, and aggregation is consistent, as we found in Chapter 4 above.

(ii) Aggregation may, however, be consistent even if all aggregation bias does not vanish. Let us suppose that for each r there exists an *exact* linear relationship between the variables x_{rs} and the corresponding aggregates x_r

$$x_{rs}(t) = \alpha_{rs} + \beta_{rs}x_r(t)$$

so that the coefficients $\beta_{qs}(q \neq r)$ and the error terms $v_{rs}(t)$ are all zero. Then aggregation bias disappears from the error term $v(t)$ of the aggregation equation (12.6). It remains true, however, that the constant term (12.6) depends on the "non-corresponding" parameters b_{rs}, and that the coefficient b_q in (12.6), although free of dependence on the "non-corresponding" parameters $b_{rs}(r \neq q)$, is not the arithmetic mean of the coefficients b_{qs}. Aggregation is nevertheless consistent; cf. above, p. 61.

(iii) Even if there is no exact linear relationship between the variables x_{rs} and the aggregate x_r, we may have the following, for each r:

$$x_{rs}(t) = \alpha_{rs} + \beta_{rs}x_r(t) + v_{rs}(t)$$

and it may be known that in each period t, the covariance of b_{rs} and $v_{rs}(t)$ is zero. Aggregation is again consistent, just as in example (ii) above. This case is analogous to Malinvaud's hypothesis that the distributions of tastes and incomes are independent; see above, pp. 66–67.

3.

But, in general, we are not so fortunate; the coefficients b_{rs} differ, and the equations (12.3) are less well-behaved. As Theil (1954, p. 14) says, with reference to equations (12.7): "Few economists will put praise on finding macroparameters (or better, statistical estimates of macro-parameters) which are mixtures of such heterogeneous components." The significance of aggregation bias, in the light of Malinvaud's proposition that the aggregate model, the aggregation procedure and the method of estimation are inter-related, is as follows. If our aggregate theory takes the form (12.6), and our aggregation procedure is to make $y = \sum_{s=1}^{n} y_s$ and $x_r = \sum_{s=1}^{n} x_{rs}$, then it is those parts of the macro-para-meters a, b_1, $\cdots$, b_m and $u(t)$ which have been defined as "aggregation bias" that will be affected by the method of statistical estimation.

This result is contained in the remarkable Theorem 7 of Theil (1954),[1] which we state as follows. Let us suppose that the parameters a, b_1, $\cdots$, b_m of the aggregate equation (12.6) are estimated, from the values of the aggregates y, x_1, $\cdots$, x_m over the periods 1, $\cdots$, T, by one of a wide class of estimating procedures.[2] Then we may write (using the symbol $\wedge$ to indicate estimates):

$$\hat{a} = A(y; x_1, \cdots, x_m \mid 1, \cdots, T)$$

$$\hat{b}_q = B_q(y; x_1, \cdots, x_m \mid 1, \cdots, T).$$

The functions A and B_q depend on the estimation procedure adopted.

Now suppose that the parameters α_{rs} and $\beta_{rs \cdot q}$ of equations (12.3) are estimated by the same procedures, so that for all q, r and s

$$\hat{\alpha}_{rs} = A(x_{rs}; x_1, \cdots, x_m \mid 1, \cdots, T)$$

$$\hat{\beta}_{rs \cdot q} = B_q(x_{rs}; x_1, \cdots, x_m \mid 1, \cdots, T).$$

Theil's Theorem 7 states that

---

[1] This theorem is stated and discussed on pp. 119 ff. and proved on pp. 183 ff. of the work cited.

[2] "We suppose that the estimation procedure is (i) linear in the variable before the semicolon, and (ii) unbiased under the condition that the disturbances of the stochastic equation have zero expectation for any values assumed by the variables behind the semicolon." *Op. cit.*, p. 119.

$$\hat{a} = \sum_{s=1}^{n} a_s + \sum_{s=1}^{n} \sum_{r=1}^{m} \hat{a}_{rs} b_{rs}$$

$$= \sum_{s=1}^{n} a_s + \sum_{s=1}^{n} \sum_{r=1}^{m} A(x_{rs}; x_1, \cdots, x_m \mid 1, \cdots, T) b_{rs} \qquad (12.8)$$

$$\hat{b}_q = \sum_{s=1}^{n} \sum_{r=1}^{m} \hat{\beta}_{rs \cdot q} b_{rs} = \sum_{s=1}^{n} \sum_{r=1}^{m} B_q(x_{rs}; x_1, \cdots, x_m \mid 1, \cdots, T) b_{rs}.$$

$$(12.9)$$

We can rewrite (12.9) as

$$\hat{b}_q = \frac{1}{n} \sum_{s=1}^{n} b_{qs} + \sum_{s=1}^{n} \left[B_q(x_{qs}; x_1, \cdots, x_m \mid 1, \cdots, T) - \frac{1}{n} \right] b_{qs}$$

$$+ \sum_{s=1}^{n} \sum_{r \neq q} B_q(x_{rs}; x_1, \cdots, x_m \mid 1, \cdots, T) b_{rs}. \qquad (12.10)$$

Similar expressions can of course be derived for the disturbances. In Theil's words (*op. cit.*, p. 121):

"The [macro] parameters estimated are sums of weighted averages of microparameters — except of course for the sum $\sum a_s$ in the macro intercept[3]—the weights being equal to the coefficients of those regression equations which are obtained when the statistical method used for the estimation of the macro equation [our (12.6)] is applied to the linear equations [our (12.3)] that describe the exogenous microvariables x_{rs} as functions of the exogenous macrovariables $x_1, \cdots, x_m$ during the period $t = 1, \cdots, T$."

Thus when the macroparameters are estimated there is a part of each $(\sum a_s$ and $(1/n) \sum b_{qs}; q = 1, \cdots, m)$ which is not affected by the statistical procedure adopted, and a part (the "aggregation bias") which is so affected.

Boot and deWit (1960) have estimated, for a model in which gross investment in large United States corporations is assumed to depend on the market value of the firm and on the value of its plant and equipment, the values of $\sum a_s$, $(1/n) \sum b_{qs}$, and the separate aggregation biases.

4.

Grunfeld and Griliches (1960) make use of the data analyzed by Boot and de Wit for a different purpose. They are concerned not with aggregation bias, but with the reliability of predictions of the aggregate

---

[3] And, we may add, except for the arithmetic means $(1/n) \sum b_{qs}$, when (12.9) is written as (12.10).

independent variable y obtained by two different methods: (a) the "aggregate" method, whereby y is predicted from an equation like our (12.6); (b) the "composite" or disaggregated method, whereby the values of the individual variables y_s are predicted from equations like our (12.2), and the results are added together.

To compare predictions obtained by these two methods, Grunfeld and Griliches make use of two measures of reliability:

(i) The "aggregate" coefficient of multiple determination R_a^2, which depends on the ratio of the variance s_a^2 of the errors of prediction of the aggregate equation (12.6)

$$u(t) = y(t) - a - \sum_{r=1}^{m} b_r x_r(t)$$

to the variance s_y^2 of $y(t)$ itself. R_a^2 is defined as

$$R_a^2 = 1 - \frac{s_a^2}{s_y^2}.$$

(ii) The "composite" coefficient of multiple determination, R_c^2, which depends on the ratio of the variance s_c^2 of the *sum* of the errors of prediction of the individual equations (12.2)

$$\sum_{s=1}^{n} u_s(t) = \sum_{s=1}^{n} \left[y_s(t) - a_s - \sum_{r=1}^{m} b_{rs} x_{rs}(t) \right]$$

to the variance of $y(t) = \sum_{s=1}^{n} y_s(t)$. R_c^2 is defined as

$$R_c^2 = 1 - \frac{s_c^2}{s_y^2}.$$

On the assumption that both $u(t)$ and $u_s(t)$ have zero expectation, we have

$$s_c^2 = \frac{1}{T} \sum_{t=1}^{T} \left[\sum_{s=1}^{n} u_s(t) \right]^2. \tag{12.11}$$

Making use of (12.2) and (12.5)

$$s_a^2 = \frac{1}{T} \sum_{t=1}^{T} [u(t)]^2$$

$$= \frac{1}{T} \sum_{t=1}^{T} \left\{ \sum_{s=1}^{n} \left[u_s(t) + \sum_{r=1}^{m} b_{rs} v_{rs}(t) \right] \right\}^2$$

$$= \frac{1}{T} \sum_{t=1}^{T} \left\{ \left[\sum_{s=1}^{n} u_s(t) \right]^2 + \left[\sum_{s=1}^{n} \sum_{r=1}^{m} b_{rs} v_{rs}(t) \right]^2 \right.$$

$$\left. + 2 \sum_{s=1}^{n} u_s(t) \sum_{w=1}^{n} \sum_{r=1}^{m} b_{rw} v_{rw}(t) \right\} \tag{12.12}$$

A comparison of (12.11) and (12.12) reveals that a necessary condition (but by no means a sufficient condition) for s_a^2 to be less than s_c^2, so that R_a^2 is greater than R_c^2 and the aggregate method gives *better* predictions, is that

$$\sum_{t=1}^{T} \left[\sum_{s=1}^{n} u_s(t) \sum_{w=1}^{n} \sum_{r=1}^{m} b_{rw} v_{rw}(t) \right] < 0.$$

The explanation given by Grunfeld and Griliches of how such a result might come about is very misleading. They refer to the case in which consumption is a function of income alone; here $m = 1$, and the index r may be suppressed. The necessary condition for $R_a^2 > R_c^2$ is then

$$\sum_{t=1}^{T} \left[\sum_{s=1}^{n} u_s(t) \sum_{w=1}^{n} b_w v_w(t) \right] < 0.$$

It is *not* sufficient for this result that $u_s(t)$ and $b_s v_s(t)$ are negatively correlated; it is $\sum u_s(t)$ and $\sum b_w v_w(t)$ that must be negatively correlated. It is not sufficient that those who have unusually high incomes (so that $v_s(t) > 0$) should "under-react" (so that $u_s(t) < 0$). What is necessary is that in the years in which those with high marginal propensities to consume tend to have unusually high incomes, so that $\sum b_w v_w(t) > 0$, there should be a general tendency for consumption to be less than that indicated by the individual equations (12.2), so that $\sum u_s(t) < 0$; and conversely that when $\sum b_w v_w(t) < 0$, $\sum u_s(t) > 0$. A simple negative correlation between $u_s(t)$ and $b_s v_s(t)$, even if it held in every year, would not give the desired result, because it would not in the least imply that $\sum u_s(t)$ and $\sum b_w v_w(t)$ had opposite signs in any year. The true necessary condition for s_a^2 to be less than s_c^2 lacks the direct plausibility of that proposed by Grunfeld and Griliches.

Be this as it may, the authors find in their study of investment that $R_a^2 = 0.926$ while $R_c^2 = 0.906$. An alternative explanation, to which they themselves attach more weight, is that the individual dependent variables y_s may depend on the aggregates $x_1, \cdots, x_m$ as well as on the individual variables x_{rs}. If this is so, to omit the aggregates $x_1, \cdots, x_m$ from the equations (12.2) is to commit a specification error when using the "composite" or disaggregated method of predicting the value of y. The "aggregate" method presumably also involves a specification error in that the variables x_{rs} are omitted from the equation (12.6). In the investment study in question, the second error appears to be less serious.

Further illustrations of the interrelated decisions involved in the aggregation problem are to be found in the discussions by Theil, (1954) and (1959), and Fisher, W. D. (1962), of simultaneous equation estimation, and in the hypothetical example presented by Malinvaud

(1956a, pp. 139–42), where the selection of an aggregation procedure is treated explicitly as a problem in decision-making under uncertainty. Malinvaud's example is taken from input-output analysis; other analyses, in the spirit of the present chapter, of aggregation problems in this field are to be found in Theil (1957) and Fisher, W. D., (1958).

CHAPTER 13

The Aggregate Production Function and the Measurement of Economic Growth

1.

In Chapters 10 and 11 the conditions for the existence of an aggregate production function were derived, for the case in which the degrees of freedom of the system were limited only by the optimal conditions of production; these optimal conditions ensured that the economy was always on the "production possibility frontier" defined by the available totals of inputs. We found that if aggregate output is to be a function homogeneous of degree one in the total inputs (as is often assumed in both non-empirical and empirical work; see for example Solow (1962)), it is necessary that the production functions for individual commodities be homogeneous of degree one, and that inputs be used in the same proportions in the production of every commodity.

Our discussion of this matter has paid little attention to aggregate output or income as a measure of welfare; welfare considerations were considered explicitly only in connection with the valuation of investment goods in terms of consumption goods. We implicitly defined an outward shift of the production possibility surface as an increase in aggregate output. Since these surfaces, under our strict aggregation conditions, are parallel hyperplanes, the proportional change or "rate of growth," as the economy moves from one hyperplane to another, can be measured unambiguously along any ray from the origin.

An example of a set of production functions satisfying our aggregation conditions is

$$y_s = A_s x_{1s}^{\alpha_1} \cdots x_{ms}^{\alpha_m}$$

with $\sum_{r=1}^{m} \alpha_r = 1$; this is the Cobb-Douglas case. But of course the exponents differ between firms. The hypothesis that the exponents for different firms differ by random disturbances from certain "true" values may be appropriate if the production functions of firms in an industry are to be aggregated into an industry production function. But the consequences of attempts to use this hypothesis in constructing an aggregate production function for the whole economy, as reported for example by Walters (1961), suggest that we should be well advised to seek additional justification for our aggregation procedures in the existence of further relationships among inputs or outputs or both, in the spirit of Chapter 8 above.

2.

It was shown in Chapter 7 (pp. 55–56 above) that if production possibility surfaces do not intersect, an outward shift of the surface may be regarded as constituting a "potential" improvement in economic welfare. But what is meant by the familiar statement that output has grown by such and such a percentage?

Consider Figure 6, which refers to only two commodities y_1 and y_2.

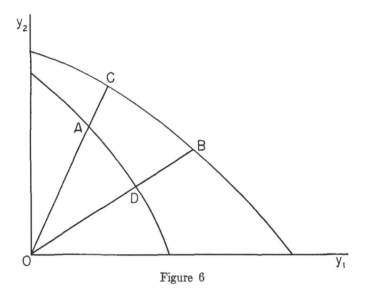

Figure 6

If the economy moves from point A on one production possibility surface to point B on another, is the rate of growth to be measured by AC/OA, DB/OD, or neither? It is clear that an unambiguous answer is possible only if production possibility surfaces are homothetic with reference to the origin.

Theoretical considerations suggest a number of circumstances which would give rise to the required homotheticity. Firstly, all individual production functions may be homogeneous of degree one, and the total inputs may all change in the same proportion. Secondly, even if all inputs do not change in the same proportion, changes in input proportions may be independent of the distribution of parameters of the individual production functions; such independence would be analogous to the independence of tastes and changes in income distribution postulated by Malinvaud (see above, pp. 66–67). The introduction of technical progress complicates matters. But it may be, thirdly, that all input totals change in the same proportion and that technical progress changes, in the same proportion for all commodities, the output obtainable from given inputs. Or, fourthly, the parameters of individual production functions as modified by technical progress may remain independent of changes in the proportions in which total inputs are available. Fifthly, it may be that some such mechanism as that envisaged by Fellner (1961) is at work; as the proportions of total inputs change, a part of technical progress may take the form of new methods designed to economize on those inputs whose relative prices are rising, so that relative costs of commodities change less than they otherwise would. Sixthly, as Hicks points out (1958, p. 148) the existence of international trade lessens the variations in the terms on which commodities are available in any single economy.

3.

It is not easy to advance beyond the purely qualitative remarks of the preceding paragraph. It would be of some interest to take a hypothetical two-input two-output model and consider the effects on the shape of the production possibility surface of differences between the production functions and changes in the proportions of total inputs. But even the usually tractable Cobb-Douglas functions are troublesome in this context. The mixture of sums and products, arithemetic means and geometric means, involved in the derivation of the equation of the production possibility surface, $F(y_1, y_2, x_1, x_2) = 0$, makes a general algebraic solution impossible.[1] The numerous cases quoted by Klein (1953, 1962) where it is legitimate to assume that arithmetic and geometric means move together, or are precisely related by virtue of a lognormal distribution (see also Chapter 8 above), are of no help in this case.

But even if production possibility surfaces are homothetic with reference to the origin, so that an unambiguous measurement of the proportional rate of growth exists in principle, a further difficulty remains. If relative prices change from one period to the next, the use of the usual quantity-indices results in a familiar bias. In Fig. 7, the movement from A to B corresponds to a "rate of growth" of $AC/OA = DB/OD$. This is underestimated by the Laspeyres ratio EB/OE and overestimated by the Paasche ratio AF/OA.[2]

---

[1] The reader who tries his hand at the problem will find himself faced, at a crucial stage, with the necessity of solving an equation of the form $ax^p + bx^q + c = 0$, where p and q are Cobb-Douglas exponents between zero and one, and in general $p \neq q$ and a, b and $c \neq 0$.

[2] The Laspeyres and Paasche ratios measure the relative values of the combinations of goods A and B at the prices ruling at A and at B respectively. Prices are here assumed to be proportional to marginal costs, which in turn reflect the slope of the production possibility surface. Throughout this chapter we disregard not only market imperfections, but also indirect taxes and subsidies.

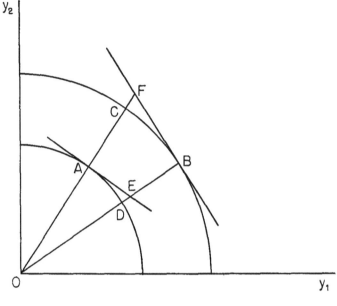

Figure 7

In view of the difficulty of writing down explicitly the equation of the production-possibility surface, it is difficult to suggest a way of eliminating this bias. We recall, however, that we have so far considered the measurement of aggregate output or income from the production side only. We shall find that to consider it also from the point of view of economic welfare leads to a possible solution of some interest.

4.

Turning therefore to a consideration of aggregate output or income as an indicator of economic welfare, we recall the results of Chapters 5 and 6. It was shown there that if individual utility functions are to be aggregated into a social utility function, which expresses "social utility" as a function of the total quantities of commodities consumed, it is necessary that each individual's indifference surfaces be homothetic with reference to the origin. In addition, the individual indifference surfaces must in general be identical—though homotheticity without identity is sufficient if we assume a constant proportional distribution of money income. As was pointed out in Chapter 7, however, these conditions are unnecessary if we are willing to assume that commodities are allocated among individuals in accordance with a social welfare function of the Bergson type. We may then interpret actual prices and quantities as sources of information about the social indifference surfaces derived from such a function. Unless these surfaces intersect—and Hicks (1958, p. 156) suggests that this is in practice unlikely—the usual Laspeyres and Paasche index numbers may be taken as indicators of the direction of changes in welfare.

It was also pointed out in Chapter 7 that if we assume that a further set of optimal conditions is satisfied—namely, that from any production possibility surface a point is always chosen so as to maximize Bergson social utility—social utility can be expressed as a function of total inputs (see p. 55 above). The result may be regarded as an aggregate production function.

5.

What then are the *welfare* implications of the use of the familiar Laspeyres and Paasche quantity indices as measures of the rate of growth of real output or income? In the special case where the aggregation conditions of Chapters 10 and 11 are satisfied, production possibility surfaces are parallel hyperplanes, relative prices are constant, and the Laspeyres and Paasche quantity indices are identical. Aggregate output or income as measured by these indices is constant at all points on a given production possibility surface. If such a measure is interpreted as an indicator of *welfare*, it is implied that the social indifference surfaces discussed in the preceding paragraph are also parallel hyperplanes, coinciding with the production possibility surfaces. This assertion may be supported by a consideration of Fig. 8.

If points *A* and *B* lie on the same production possibility surface, and each represents a maximization of social utility subject to the constraints imposed by the production surface, then the social indifference surface must coincide with the production surface between *A* and *B*. For if social indifference surfaces were smoothly convex to the origin, as they are usually drawn, the choice of both *A* and *B* would imply that the indifference surfaces intersected, as in Fig. 8; such intersections are of course inconsistent with the expression of utility as a function of quantities consumed. It may be argued, however, that movements along a given production possibility surface are seldom observed, and that we need consider only movements like that from *A* to *C* in Fig. 8, from one production surface to another. But if indifference surfaces are smoothly convex to the origin at *A* and at *C*, and relative quantities are different, the measurement of percentage changes in output is ambiguous. An unambiguous measurement of the percentage rate of growth of income, in the "welfare" sense we are now considering, requires social indifference surfaces to be homothetic with reference to the origin. The problem is exactly analogous to that illustrated by Fig. 6 above.

Hicks suggests (1958, p. 148) that relative prices vary less over time

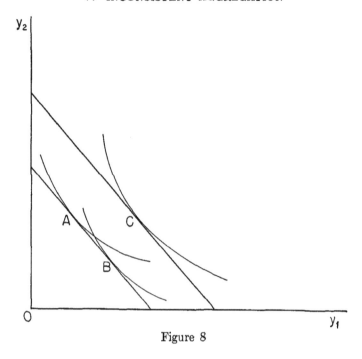

Figure 8

than relative quantities. This suggestion leads us to propose the following interpretation of the measurement of real output or income by means of the usual Laspeyres and Paasche quantity indices. Such measurement may be regarded as based on the hypothesis that there exists a set of "normal" relative prices of commodities for an economy during the period under consideration. Actual relative prices diverge from their normal values in a random fashion, and differences between the Laspeyres and Paasche indices reflect these divergences. This hypothesis would seem to require that there should be a single quantity-index for the period, and that the price-weights to be used in it should be derived from a statistical estimate of the "normal" prices.

It remains true, however, that a measurement of welfare based on the hypothesis of constant relative prices implies *either* that social indifference surfaces are hyperplanes, at least within the observed range of variation of relative quantities, *or* that no unambiguous statement of proportional changes in income or output is possible. The former alternative implies that within the relevant range commodities are perfect substitutes, and that quantities consumed are indeterminate. This of course becomes less plausible the wider are the variations in relative quantities.

The measurement of percentage changes in real income or output will therefore give rise to less difficulty the closer is the approximation to proportionality of *both* prices *and* quantities. If both social indifference surfaces and production possibility surfaces are roughly homothetic with reference to the origin, both prices and quantities will tend to move together. And as we saw earlier, production possibility surfaces will be homothetic if individual production functions are homogeneous of degree one and the total available quantities of different types of input change in the same proportion.

6.

The argument of the preceding paragraph leads to the conclusion that the measurement of economic growth and the estimation of an aggregate production function are easy in a steadily progressive economy, all of whose parts are growing at the same rate! This somewhat banal result does suggest, however, two concluding comments. The first draws attention to an interesting recent paper on aggregation by Simon and Ando; the second suggests that the use of a different type of quantity-index will circumvent some of the difficulties encountered earlier in this chapter.

Simon and Ando (1961) postulate an economic system with a simple dynamic structure, and call attention to three phases in its development, distinguished by the relative movements of the variables. In the first phase, it is only fortuitously that variables move in proportion to each other. In the second phase, groups of variables emerge whose members tend to move proportionally. In the third phase, as the final equilibrium of the system is approached, all variables in all groups tend to move proportionally.

There is no doubt that experiments with various kinds of dynamic structure, along the lines of Simon and Ando's article,[3] should play an important part in further investigations of the implications of restrictions of the degrees of freedom of a system (e.g. the proportionality of members of a group of variables) for the possibilities of aggregation. With reference to the aggregate production function, the properties of Simon and Ando's second phase may permit aggregation in parts of the system. (The assumption that the pattern of relative wage-rates is relatively stable, for example, permits a natural way of aggregating different types of labour).

But the conclusion of the argument of this chapter so far is that if the usual type of index of real output is to be used, and if measurements of rates of growth are not to be ambiguous, we must be in Simon and Ando's third phase, the "steadily progressive economy," rather than the second.

---

[3] Their ideas have been pursued in Ando and Fisher (1963).

7.

Our suggestion for an alternative type of quantity-index is based on the replacement of the hypothesis that relative *prices* fluctuate about certain normal values by the hypothesis that the proportions in which expenditure is divided among commodities fluctuate about certain normal values.[4] If expenditure proportions are constant, actual purchases can be thought of as the result of maximizing a social utility function of the form

$$U = y_1^{a_1} y_2^{a_2} \cdots y_n^{a_n}$$

where $a_1, \cdots, a_n$ are the expenditure proportions. The utility function is homogeneous of degree one since $\sum_{s=1}^{n} a_s = 1$, and social indifference surfaces are homothetic and smoothly convex to the origin; this is, of course, the Cobb-Douglas function discussed elsewhere in this volume. It can be shown (cf. pp. 27, 58 above) that if total expenditure and prices in two situations are E', p_1', $\cdots$, p_n' and E'', p_1'', $\cdots$, p_n'', then

$$\frac{U''}{U'} = \frac{E''}{E'} \prod_{s=1}^{n} \left(\frac{p_s'}{p_s''}\right)^{a_s}.$$

To obtain a measure of the proportional change in U, expenditure must be deflated by a price index which is a weighted geometric mean of prices—the weights are the expenditure proportions. By assuming that from any production possibility surface that point is selected which maximizes U as defined, we can express U as a function of total inputs, and thus obtain an aggregate production function.[5]

The advantage of this measure is that changing relative prices do not lead to bias. Even if social indifference surfaces are homothetic with reference to the origin, as in Fig. 9 (which is analogous to Fig.7), the unambiguous rate of growth $AC/OA = DB/OD$ is overestimated by the usual Laspeyres index as EB/OE and underestimated by the Paasche index as AF/OA. If the utility function is of the Cobb-Douglas type, deflation of total expenditure by the geometric-mean price index defined above will yield the "true" value.

---

[4] This suggestion is reminiscent of the "constant utility index of the cost of living" of Rubin and Klein (1948).

[5] Of the specific problems discussed in Chapters 10 and 11, the questions of valuing investment goods in terms of consumption goods, and of allowing for quality changes in consumption goods, are still present, but create no new difficulties when real output is measured in the manner now proposed. If capital goods, regarded as *inputs*, are grouped together into a single index of capital, or into a number of indices of different types of capital goods, there must still exist, for each group of capital goods, a function, homogeneous of degree one in the items in the group, which appears in each individual production function; similar remarks apply to labour inputs. And the capital goods in any one group must all wear out at the same rate, as in Chapters 10 and 11.

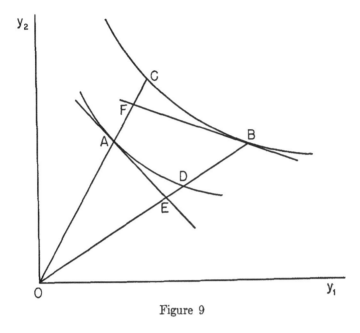

Figure 9

The proposed measure depends on the hypothesis of constant "normal" expenditure proportions for its justification; this hypothesis may be unsatisfactory over long periods: it is inconsistent with Engel's Law, for example.[6] The usual measures of real income depend in the same way, we have suggested, on the hypothesis of constant "normal" price-ratios among commodities. They imply in addition, however, *either* that social indifference surfaces are hyperplanes in the range of variation of relative quantities, *or* that they are not homothetic with reference to the origin, which makes statements about proportional rates of growth inherently ambiguous. It would be instructive to make a comparison of measured rates of growth, and of estimated aggregate production functions, computed according to these two hypotheses.

[6] Other more complicated utility functions could of course be postulated, requiring the use of more complicated indices, which would not share the Cobb-Douglas function's disadvantage of resting on the somewhat shaky hypothesis of constant "normal" expenditure proportions.

Part VI
CONCLUSION

CHAPTER 14

Summary: Factors in the Selection of an Aggregation Procedure

In Part II of this volume we considered the grouping of variables in a single utility or production function. A part of the interest of this problem lies in the possibility of breaking down the process, whereby quantities of elementary commodities or inputs are determined, into two stages. To the extent that the interest of the investigator is directed primarily to these "elementary" quantities, the aggregates used are devices to simplify the analysis; to use a term of Malinvaud (1956a), they are "representative" aggregates. The aggregation problem of input-output analysis, in one of its aspects, may be similarly interpreted.

But this is not the type of problem with which we have been mainly concerned. In Parts III–V, we took a set of production, utility or demand functions, each stating a relationship between a dependent variable and a number of independent variables. We considered the replacement of these micro-relations by a single macro-relation between an aggregate dependent variable and a number of aggregate independent variables, with the purpose of predicting the value of the former from the values of the latter. (Aggregation problems of simultaneous-equations estimation have been analyzed by Theil (1954) and (1959) and Fisher, W. D. (1962)). Part II is concerned in part with this problem, in that the demand functions of an individual or firm for elementary commodities or inputs are aggregated into group demand functions with group price-indices as their arguments. In the aggregation of the utility and production functions of different individuals, firms and industries, which occupies Parts III–V of this volume, the "commodities" and "inputs" which appear in the micro-relations are in practice almost inevitably the result of grouping.

The way in which the aggregate dependent variable is related to the dependent micro-variables is determined by considerations other than the desire for accurate prediction. The choice is imposed upon the investigator by the nature of the economic problem in question; he would be interested, for example, in the sum, rather than the product, of quantities of sugar consumed by households. There may, however, be some doubt about the most appropriate way of defining such a concept as "aggregate output", as the discussion in Chapter 13 shows.

The choice of the type and degree of aggregation of independent variables, however, is to be determined by the balancing of two types of cost—the cost of using variables which are numerous and/or difficult to estimate, and the costs associated with the unsatisfactory predictions which may result if the number of variables is small.

For each way of aggregating the independent variables, and for each type of macro-relation assumed to hold among aggregates, it is possible in principle to derive the conditions on the micro-relations which are necessary and sufficient for consistent aggregation. These conditions can be derived (as in Chapter 5 and the early part of Chapter 9) on the assumption that the movements of the independent micro-variables are unrestricted. They can be derived (as in Chapters 6–7, 10–11, and 13) on the assumption that the economic system conforms to certain optimal conditions. And they can be derived (as in Chapter 8, the latter part of Chapter 9, and part of Chapter 13) on the assumption that certain other relationships, perhaps expressible by means of probability distribution functions, exist among the independent micro-variables, or between these variables and the parameters of the micro-relations (see, for example, the hypotheses concerning the distribution of incomes considered in Chapter 8).

But the interest of the investigator is assumed to be directed to prediction, which involves statistical methods. The extent to which the failure of the strict conditions for consistent aggregation will lead to unsatisfactory predictions can be discovered only by considering these conditions in relation to the statistical procedure used to estimate the macro-relation. Less has been done on this aspect of the aggregation problem than on the conditions for consistent aggregation themselves. In Chapter 12 some references were given to work that has been done in this area, and the concepts of "aggregation bias" in the estimation of the parameters of the macro-relation, and of "aggregation error" in the prediction of the aggregate dependent variable, were illustrated.

There remains the weighing of the two types of cost referred to above. A decision as to the appropriate aggregation procedure must depend on the utility to the investigator of the uncertain outcomes of alternative procedures. We conclude that the aggregation problem is properly regarded as a part of statistical decision theory, and that in this direction lie the best prospects for fruitful development.

List of References

The titles of journals referred to more than once in this bibliography are abbreviated as follows:

American Economic Review	AER
Econometrica	Em
Economic Journal	EJ
International Economic Review	IER
Oxford Economic Papers	OEP
Quarterly Journal of Economics	QJE
Review of Economic Studies	REStud
Review of Economics and Statistics	REStat

Adelman, Irma, and Lobo, O., (1956): "Some observations on full employment vs. full capacity," *AER*, vol. 46, June 1956, pp. 412–19.

Adelman, Irma, and Griliches, Z. (1961): "On an index of quality change," *Journal of the American Statistical Association*, vol. 56, Sept. 1961, pp. 535–48.

Aitchison, J., and Brown, J. A. C., (1957): *The Lognormal Distribution*, Cambridge, England, 1957.

Allen, R. G. D. (1956): *Mathematical Economics*, London, 1956.

Ando, A. and Fisher, F. M. (1963): "Near-decomposability, partition and aggregation, and the relevance of stability discussions," *IER*, vol. 4, Jan. 1963, pp. 53–67.

Ando, A: *see* Simon and Ando (1961).

Ara, K. (1959): "The aggregation problem in input-output analysis," *Em*, vol. 27, Apr. 1959, pp. 257–62.

Arrow, K. J. (1951): *Social Choice and Individual Values*, New York, 1951.

Balderston, Judith B., and Whitin, T. M. (1954): "Aggregation in the input-output model," in *Economic Activity Analysis* (O. Morgenstern, editor), New York, 1954.

Boot, J. C. G., and Wit, G. M. de (1960): "Investment demand: an empirical contribution to the aggregation problem," *IER*, vol. 1, Jan. 1960, pp. 3–30.

Brown, J. A. C: *see* Aitchison and Brown (1957).

Denison, E. F. (1957): "Theoretical aspects of quality change, capital consumption, and net capital formation," in *Problems of Capital Formation* (Conference on Research in Income and Wealth: Studies in Income and Wealth, vol. 19), Princeton, 1957, pp. 215–61.

Divisia, F. (1925–26): "L'indice monétaire et la théorie de la monnaie,"

Revue d'Economie Politique, vol. 29, July–Aug. 1925, pp. 842–61, Sept.–Oct. 1925, pp. 980–1008, Nov.–Dec. 1925, pp. 1121–51; vol. 30, Jan.–Feb. 1926, pp. 49–81.

Domar, E. D. (1953): "Depreciation, replacement and growth," *EJ,* vol. 63, Mar. 1953, pp. 1–32.

Dorfman, R., Samuelson, P. A., and Solow, R. M. (1958): *Linear Programming and Economic Analysis,* New York, 1958.

Farrell, M. J. (1954): "Some aggregation problems in demand analysis," *REStud,* vol. 21 (3), 1953–54, pp. 193–203.

Fei, J. C. H. (1956): "A fundamental theorem for the aggregation problem of input-output analysis," *Em,* vol. 24, Oct. 1956, pp. 400–12.

Fellner, W. (1961): "Two propositions in the theory of induced innovations," *EJ,* vol. 71, June 1961, pp. 305–08.

Fisher, F. M.: *see* Ando and Fisher, F. M. (1963).

Fisher, I. (1922): *The Making of Index Numbers,* Boston and New York, 1922.

Fisher, W. D. (1958): "Criteria for aggregation in input-output analysis," *REStat,* vol. 40, Aug. 1958, pp. 250–60.

—— (1962): "Optimal aggregation in multi-equation prediction models," *Em,* vol. 30, Oct. 1962, pp. 744–69.

Friedman, M. (1957): *A Theory of the Consumption Function,* Princeton, 1957.

Frisch, R. (1936): "Annual survey of general economic theory: the problem of index numbers," *Em,* vol. 4, Jan. 1936, pp. 1–38.

Goldsmith, R. W. (1961): "Comment," in *Output, Input and Productivity Measurement* (Conference on Research in Income and Wealth: Studies in Income and Wealth, vol. 25) Princeton, 1961, pp. 444–46.

Gordon, R. A. (1961): "Price changes: consumers' and capital goods," *AER,* vol. 51, Dec. 1961, pp. 937–57.

Gorman, W. M. (1953): "Community preference fields," *Em,* vol. 21, Jan. 1953, pp. 63–80.

—— (1959a): "Separable utility and aggregation," *Em,* vol. 27, July 1959, pp. 469–81.

—— (1959b): "The empirical implications of a utility tree: a further comment," *Em,* vol. 27, July 1959, p. 489.

—— (1963): "Additive logarithmic preferences: a further note," *REStud,* vol. 30 (1), Feb. 1963, pp. 56–62.

Green, H. A. J. (1960): "Growth models, capital and stability," *EJ,* vol. 70, Mar. 1960, pp. 57–73.

—— (1962): "A note on the measurement of capital," *Canadian*

Journal of Economics and Political Science, vol. 28, May 1962, pp. 281–82.

Griliches, Z.: *see* Adelman and Griliches (1961) *and* Grunfeld and Griliches (1960).

Grunfeld, Yehuda, and Griliches, Z. (1960): "Is aggregation necessarily bad?" *REStat,* vol. 42, Feb. 1960, pp. 1–13.

Hatanaka, M. (1952): "A note on consolidation within a Leontief system," *Em,* vol. 20, Apr. 1952, pp. 301–03.

Hicks, J. R. (1946): *Value and Capital,* second edition, Oxford, 1946.

————— (1958): "The measurement of real income," *OEP,* new series, vol. 10, June 1958, pp. 125–62.

————— (1961): "The measurement of capital in relation to the measurement of other economic aggregates," in *The Theory of Capital* (F. A. Lutz, chairman of programme committee; D. C. Hague, editor), London, 1961, pp. 18–31.

Hood, W. C. (1952): "Some problems of aggregation," (paper delivered to the Canadian Political Science Association, June 1952; unpublished).

Houthakker, H. S. (1960): "Additive Preferences," *Em,* vol. 28, Apr. 1960, pp. 244–57.

Houthakker, H. S.: *see* Prais and Houthakker (1955).

Hurwicz, L. (1952): "Aggregation in macroeconomic models," (abstract), *Em,* vol. 20, July 1952, pp. 489–90.

Kaldor, N. (1956): "Alternative theories of distribution," *REStud,* vol. 23 (2), 1955–6, pp. 83–100.

————— (1961): contribution to "The discussion of Professor Hicks' paper," in *The Theory of Capital* (F. A. Lutz, chairman of programme committee; D. C. Hague, editor), London, 1961, pp. 304–05.

Klein, L. R. (1946a): "Macroeconomics and the theory of rational behavior," *Em,* vol. 14, Apr. 1946, pp. 93–108.

————— (1946b): "Remarks on the theory of aggregation," *Em,* vol. 14, Oct. 1946, pp. 303–12.

————— (1953): *Econometrics,* Evanston, Illinois, 1953.

————— (1962): *An Introduction to Econometrics,* New York, 1962.

Klein, L. R.: *see* Rubin and Klein (1948).

Koopmans, T. C. (1960): "Stationary ordinal utility and impatience," *Em,* vol. 28, Apr. 1960, pp. 287–309.

Leontief, W. W. (1936): "Composite commodities and the problem of index numbers," *Em,* vol. 4, Jan. 1936, pp. 39–59.

————— (1947a): "A note on the interrelation of subsets of independent variables of a continuous function with continuous first derivatives," *Bulletin of the American Mathematical Society*, vol. 53, 1947, pp. 343–50.

—— (1947b): "Introduction to a theory of the internal structure of functional relationships," *Em*, vol. 15, Oct. 1947, pp. 361–73.

Lobo, O.: see Adelman and Lobo (1956).

McManus, M. (1956a): "General consistent aggregation in Leontief models," *Yorkshire Bulletin of Economic Research*, vol. 8, June 1956, pp. 28–48.

—— (1956b): "On Hatanaka's note on consolidation," *Em*, vol. 24, Oct. 1956, pp. 482–87.

Malinvaud, E. (1956a): "L'agrégation dans les modèles économiques," *Cahiers du Séminaire d'Econométrie*, no. 4, Paris, 1956, pp. 69–146.

—— (1956b): "Aggregation problems in input-output models," in *The Structural Interdependence of the Economy* (T. Barna, editor), New York, 1956, pp. 187–202.

May, K. O. (1946): "The aggregation problem for a one-industry model," *Em*, vol. 14, Oct. 1946, pp. 285–98.

——(1947): "Technological change and aggregation," *Em*, vol. 15, Jan. 1947, pp. 51–63.

Meade, J. E. (1961): *A Neo-Classical Theory of Economic Growth*, London, 1961.

Morishima, M. (1961): "A historical note on Professor Sono's theory of separability," *IER*, vol. 2, Sept. 1961, pp. 272–75.

Nataf, A. (1948): "Sur la possibilité de construction de certains macro-modèles," *Em*, vol. 16, July 1948, pp. 232–44.

—— (1953): "Sur des questions d'agrégation en économétrie," *Publications de l'Institut de Statistique de l'Université de Paris*, vol. 2, Fasc. 4, 1953.

Nataf, A., and Roy, R. (1948): "Remarques et suggestions relatives aux nombres-indices," *Em*, vol. 16, Oct. 1948, pp. 330–46.

Pearce, I. F. (1961): "An exact method of consumer demand analysis," *Em*, vol. 29, Oct. 1961, pp. 499–516.

Peston, M. H. (1959): "A view of the aggregation problem," *REStud*, vol. 27 (1), 1959–60, pp. 58–64.

Prais, S. J., and Houthakker, H. S. (1955): *The Analysis of Family Budgets*, Cambridge, England, 1955.

Robinson, Joan (1954): "The production function and the theory of capital," *REStud*, vol. 21 (2), 1953–54, pp. 81–106.

—— (1956): *The Accumulation of Capital*, London, 1956.

Roy, R.: see Nataf and Roy (1948).

Rubin, H. and Klein, L. R. (1948): "A constant utility index of the cost of living," *REStud*, vol. 15 (2), 1947–48, pp. 84–7.

Samuelson, P. A. (1947): *Foundations of Economic Analysis*, Cambridge, Mass., 1947.

——(1950): "Evaluation of real national income," *OEP*, new series, vol. 2, Jan. 1950, pp. 1–29.

—— (1951): "Abstract of a theorem concerning substitutability in open Leontief models," in *Activity Analysis of Production and Allocation* (T. C. Koopmans, editor), New York, 1951, pp. 142–46.

—— (1956): "Social indifference curves," *QJE*, vol. 70, Feb. 1956, pp. 1–22.

—— (1961): "The evaluation of 'social income': capital formation and wealth," in *The Theory of Capital*, (F. A. Lutz, chairman of programme committee; D. C. Hague, editor), London, 1961, pp. 32–57.

—— (1962): "Parable and realism in the theory of capital: the surrogate production function," *REStud*, vol. 29 (3), June 1962, pp. 193–206

Samuelson, P. A.: *see* Dorfman, Samuelson, and Solow (1958).

Scitovsky, T. (1942): "A reconsideration of the theory of tariffs," *REStud*, vol. 9 (2), 1941–2, pp. 89–110.

Simon, H. A., and Ando, A. (1961): "Aggregation of variables in dynamic systems," *Em*, vol. 29, Apr. 1961, pp. 111–38.

Solow, R. M. (1956a): "A contribution to the theory of economic growth," *QJE*, vol. 70, Feb. 1956, pp. 65–94.

—— (1956b): "The production function and the theory of capital," *REStud*, vol. 23 (2), 1955–56, pp. 101–08.

—— (1957): "Technical change and the aggregate production function," *REStat*, vol. 39, Aug. 1957, pp. 312–20.

—— (1962): "Technical progress, capital formation, and economic growth," in *American Economic Association: Papers and Proceedings*, May 1962, pp. 76–86.

Solow, R. M.: *see* Dorfman, Samuelson and Solow (1958).

Sono, M. (1961): "The effect of price changes on the demand and supply of separable goods," *IER*, vol. 2, Sept. 1961, pp. 239–71.

Sraffa, P. (1960): *Production of Commodities by Means of Commodities*, Cambridge, England, 1960.

Stone, R. (1954): *The Measurement of Consumers' Expenditure and Behaviour in the United Kingdom*, 1920–38, Cambridge, England, 1954.

—— (1956): *Quantity and Price Indices in National Accounts*, Paris, 1956.

Strotz, R. (1957): "The empirical implications of a utility tree," *Em*, vol. 25, Apr. 1957, pp. 269–80.

—— (1959): "The utility tree: a correction and further appraisal," *Em*, vol. 27, July 1959, pp. 482–88.

Swan, T. W. (1956): "Economic growth and capital accumulation," *Economic Record*, vol. 32, Nov. 1956, pp. 334–61.

Theil, H. (1954): *Linear Aggregation of Economic Relations*, Amsterdam, 1954.

—— (1957): "Linear aggregation in input-output analysis," *Em*, vol. 25, Jan. 1957, pp. 111–22.

—— (1959): "The aggregation implications of identifiable structural macrorelations," *Em*, vol. 27, Jan. 1959, pp. 14–29.

Tobin, J. (1950): "A statistical demand function for food in the U.S.A.," *Journal of the Royal Statistical Society*, Series A, vol. 113, Part 2, 1950, pp. 113–41.

Ulmer, M. J. (1949): *The Economic Theory of Cost of Living Index Numbers*, New York, 1949.

Walters, A. A. (1961): "Some notes on the Cobb-Douglas production function," *Metroeconomica*, vol. 13, Dec. 1961, pp. 121–38.

Whitin, T. M.: *see* Balderston and Whitin (1954).

Wit, G. M. de: *see* Boot and de Wit (1960).

Wolff, P. de (1941): "Income elasticity of demand, a micro-economic and a macro-economic interpretation," *EJ*, vol. 51, Apr. 1941, pp. 140–45.

Index

Milton Keynes UK
Ingram Content Group UK Ltd.
UKHW030737141024
449609UK00006B/165

9 780691 624914